Introduction

REPRESENTATION, REALISM & FANTASY

Teaching Notes

This pack follows **Reading Films – Key Concepts for Analysing Film and Television** in the series, *Moving Image Media in English*. Like *Reading Films*, it supports Key Stage 4 requirements of the National Curriculum in England for work on 'moving image media', including the media component of GCSE English. It provides materials to help students study complete films and film extracts.

Although the awarding bodies have different interpretations of National Curriculum requirements, most examine the knowledge and understanding of media through coursework. Suggested areas of exploration are:

- The social and media context of material;
- Significant achievements within a genre;
- How language is used, presentational devices, the use of visual images for specific emotive, persuasive, or perceptual devices.

The pack primarily deals with films that can be linked with the study of Key Stage 4 English and English Literature. Films covered include several adaptations of literary works. All the films deal with social, historical or cultural issues and each can be 'read' on a number of different levels inviting an audience to make connections with the deeper social questions that are raised. The pack is divided into three sections:

- Unit 1: Representation and Genre
- Unit 2: Social Context, Metaphor and Allegory
- Case Studies.

AIMS AND OBJECTIVES

The main aims of the pack are to develop students' understanding of:

- Key moving image concepts such as **representation** and **genre**;
- The ways in which representation and genre affect our 'reading' of particular film and television texts;
- Key literary concepts such as **metaphor** and **allegory**;
- The ways in which these ideas can be applied to the study of film and television texts.

The pack has been designed to cover both National Curriculum and English GCSE requirements, enabling students to produce a substantial piece of coursework that demonstrates the ability to analyse and review moving image texts which can be assessed in relation to EN3 (Writing) and EN1 (Speaking and Listening). It is also designed to deepen the understanding of style, structure, language and genre while consolidating the importance of social and historical influences upon texts.

USING THE PACK

The ideas in this pack can be applied to a wide range of films. However, we focus on four films. Two of these films, *Kes* and *Pleasantville*, have been used before, in *Reading Films*, and you can use them again to deepen students' understanding and appreciation of these texts, or can focus on the other films. To use this pack effectively it is important to focus on at least two films.

- *The Crucible* (US, 1996)
- *To Kill a Mockingbird* (US, 1962)
- *Kes* (UK, 1969)
- *Pleasantville* (US, 1998.)

In addition, there are case studies of:

- *The Wizard of Oz* (US, 1939)
- *Buffy the Vampire Slayer* – ongoing TV series.

You will need to have the films and episodes from the television series you are studying on video or DVD. They are available on VHS or DVD at the time of publication and have been chosen because they are suitable for schools (all are certificate '12'). Further appropriate titles are suggested in the **Resources** section.

There is a wealth of information in this pack and you may not need to use all the material to fulfil all the aims. You are, however, strongly advised to read through the whole pack and to select what is suitable and manageable for your circumstances. It would be useful to cover **Unit 1 – Reading Films** in the first pack in this series, *Reading Films*, before tackling one of these units, as it provides an appropriate framework for the understanding and analysis of film texts.

Careful planning of how you use chosen texts at the beginning of the two year Key Stage 4 course will enable you to cover a range of areas. It is important to remember that the films recommended in this teaching pack do not replace literary texts, but they can make a significant contribution in terms of the consolidation of learning, enhancing students' understanding and improving their analytical skills.

UNITS

Each unit includes **Teaching Notes** – brief notes and guidelines for

THE CRUCIBLE

teachers, and **Student Notes and Activities**. Teachers should work with students on the student notes in a classroom context, and in conjunction with viewing extracts from the selected films. Activities are suggested to help the students understand important concepts and engage with the material more effectively. They are designed to be tackled by students individually or in small groups while making reference back to the student notes.

CASE STUDIES

Following the two main units in the pack, **Representation and Genre** and **Metaphor and Allegory**, are six case studies. The first three look at adaptations of the literary texts *The Crucible* by Arthur Miller, *To Kill a Mockingbird* by Harper Lee and *A Kestrel for a Knave* (1968) by Barry Hines (adapted as *Kes*). These case studies are designed to enable students to extend and deepen their study of metaphor, allegory, genre and representation. *Pleasantville* links with both *The Crucible* and *To Kill a Mockingbird* in terms of themes, social comment and the use of metaphor and allegory. It also introduces ideas about realism and fantasy which are explored in Unit 1. Work on *The Wizard of Oz* and *Buffy the Vampire Slayer* extends the study of allegory in fantasy texts.

BACKGROUND INFORMATION

The work in the pack requires a fair amount of background knowledge. Where space permits we have included appropriate material. In some cases it may be necessary to check the Student Notes if a term is not explained in the case

study (eg America in the 1950s). Some of the case studies lend themselves to much wider research projects that could utilise the internet or appropriate links to other subjects.

A SCHEME OF WORK

A minimum scheme of work, leading to a substantial piece of coursework, should include Unit 1 or 2, followed by activities selected from one or more of the case studies. This will enable you to include a wide range of activities with a clear focus, for example, allegory, with scope for comparing different texts. The Student Notes explain the concepts introduced through the films and are designed to enable students to analyse films effectively. The activities allow the students to become familiar with concepts and encourage initial analysis in relation to the film texts. The case studies provide background information on each film and encourage students to deepen their analysis of social, historical and cultural contexts alongside specific aspects of film form. It is envisaged that these case studies will provide the necessary stimulus and information needed in order to enable students across the ability range to produce a substantial piece of coursework for English GCSE.

ESSAY QUESTIONS

GCSE students could select from the essay questions provided here to produce a substantial piece of work, building on previous classroom activities.

MEDIA AND LITERARY TEXTS

The National Curriculum and GCSE specifications explicitly require 'a review of the medium itself' so it is

not acceptable to replace the study of a literary text with film adaptation, or vice versa. Nevertheless, with time constraints in mind and the possibilities of an 'enhanced learning experience', we have chosen texts that allow a 'cross-over' of learning and understanding with other areas of the National Curriculum for English and GCSE English Literature:

■ *Kes* was adapted for the screen by Barry Hines from his own novel, *A Kestrel for a Knave*. If you are using *A Kestrel for a Knave* for a post-1914 text for English Literature, you may also find it useful and illuminating to consider the ways in which the rich symbolism of the novel and the metaphorical importance of the kestrel are expressed through the language of film.

■ *To Kill a Mockingbird* was adapted from a novel written in 1960 by Harper Lee, which could also be studied as part of the post-1914 English Literature requirements. Like the kestrel in *A Kestrel for a Knave*, the mockingbird has a central, metaphorical importance in the novel and an analysis of the use of allegory and metaphor within the film's language should allow a deeper understanding of both the novel and the film.

■ Arthur Miller adapted his play *The Crucible*, written in 1953, for the screen in 1996. In an article written during the making of the film he highlighted the importance of film in reaching a wide audience. He also stressed the continuing social relevance of this allegorical work. The study of his adaptation should raise interesting questions about the contemporary relevance of this text both in its play form and as a film. The work on allegory is designed to help illuminate a difficult concept and enrich the students' understanding of its use in literature and film. At the heart of the work lies the understanding that many texts can be read on different levels, and that meaning can change across time and according to social and cultural context.

DIFFERENTIATION

We have tried to write at a level that is accessible to a wide range of students and to provide ideas for questions and activities which could be adapted to suit all student needs, but we also assume that teachers will mediate the material for their students. Much of the material in the pack has been 'piloted' in a variety of schools in Cumbria, Leeds and Calderdale. Some of these schools had mixed ability groups; some used a system of setting. The work was equally successful across the ability range and several teachers have observed that differentiating by outcome rather than input enabled all their students to fulfil their potential far more effectively.

SCREENING FILMS

An important issue for teachers is likely to be the time taken up by screenings. It is important that students watch the films they are studying straight through. Films are constructed for an audience watching a complete narrative at one sitting and film language works best on a big screen with cinema sound. There is enormous value in taking students to a cinema screening (details of how to negotiate with cinemas for educational screenings are given in the **Resources** section).

The next best option is to arrange video or DVD projection within the classroom, during the lesson or a lunch hour, if necessary broken into two or three parts to fit into the time. Some students may be able to watch films or video outside class time, either at an after-school screening, or at home. It is useful to come to an arrangement with your librarian, so that at least one spare

PLEASANTVILLE

copy of the film you are studying is available in the library, and can be loaned out to students on a nightly basis when they embark on their coursework. This will allow them to spend time focusing upon particular scenes for analysis and will also ensure equality of access for all students.

The Student Notes and Activities invite students to watch specific sequences of the focus films, and you need to be prepared for this, lining up the specific sequences before the start of the lesson and/or making a note of their start time on the video.

ICT

The use of the internet to research films, as recommended in the Student Notes, as well as word processing software to write up their projects will give students useful experience of ICT.

TEACHING TECHNIQUES

The student activities in the units draw on a range of well-tested basic teaching techniques presented in *Moving Images in the Classroom* (bfi 2001). These techniques are applicable to any moving image text and the ideas for activities in the pack can be developed for use with a wide range of other films and television programmes. Some of the techniques require attention to technology in the classroom.

- Analysis of film language requires students to look carefully at the constituents of the visual image. Ideally, you need a VCR with a good still image function for the classroom. Unfortunately, it is difficult to get most classroom

VCRs to do this and endless stopping of the tape may damage both tape and the VCR. Running through a short sequence two, or three times is often sufficient for students to remember particular images and make notes. It is important to have a VCR with a remote control for this kind of work and a good timer for finding particular scenes. DVD offers perfect still images, without any fear of damaging the disc, and this format is becoming increasingly attractive for the classroom – especially when useful additional material offers new ways into the analysis of film. You can also find suitable stills for student work on the internet. http://www.cinema.com is a useful source of large, good quality images from current films on release.

- In order to explore how sound and image complement each other and expose how film narratives are constructed, it is useful to be able to play video sequences without sound or with different sound, played on a sound system. To play the soundtrack without showing the images you can turn round the TV monitor or cover it with a cloth, but the sound is better if you can push it through a separate amplifier.

- The development of digital media technologies, such as DVD, is making such activities more manageable in school, as well as presenting new possibilities. Your school's computer network may enable students to access a source of video stills and short sequences. This presents the possibility of digitising short sequences from films under analysis and re-editing them as a means of exploring story structure.

To develop your own understanding of film language and how films construct meaning we strongly recommend you work through the interactive CD-ROM *An Introduction to Film Language*. It is available for £27.99 and can be ordered from *bfi* Education Resources – Tel. 0870 241 3764.

BASIC TEACHING TECHNIQUES

The following extract is taken from *Moving Images in the Classroom, A secondary teachers' guide to using film and television* (*bfi* 2000). The whole guide can be downloaded from www.bfi.org.uk/education.

We all know how frustrating it can be to show a video to pupils and get nothing much back in response apart from 'it was boring' or 'I liked the bit where…'. And what kinds of question can you ask of pupils other than 'look out for…'? Using video more productively is not just a matter of knowing some technical terms – though these can help. It depends upon recognising that the moving image has a complex and dense language of its own that we have all learned to 'read' with such ease while not necessarily being aware of our own skills.

The eight basic techniques described on the following pages are designed to help you unravel the codes and conventions of the moving image, and enable you to use a wider range of film and video texts in the classroom. As you and your pupils unpack the layers of meaning, you will be helping them to develop their general skills as more critical, attentive and knowledgeable readers of the moving image. The techniques are not age-specific. You could use any of them with any age-group depending on the topic in hand, the moving image text you want to base them on, and how far you want to follow through each activity. But you may feel that Techniques 7 and 8 are inherently more sophisticated and thus more appropriate for Key Stage 4.

The first three techniques concentrate on the language of the moving image. They offer you ways of encouraging pupils to see how everything in a moving image text is saying something, and contributing in some way to its overall meaning. Technique 1, **Freeze Frame**, concentrates on the visual language of moving images. Technique 2, **Sound and Image**, helps pupils see how important sound is in the interpretation of moving image texts. Technique 3, **Spot the Shots**, draws their attention to the editing process. Any of these techniques can be used from time to time in very short sessions to build up pupils' critical awareness of how moving image texts work, and your confidence in using the technique to develop more critical and thoughtful ways of working with moving images.

The next two techniques, **Top and Tail** and **Attracting Audiences**, deal with the ways in which moving image texts are produced and circulated to audiences. Whatever your subject area, it is important to point out to pupils that any moving image text need not necessarily be taken at face value. They should think about where a film or TV programme comes from and whose interests it may be serving, if they are to use its information critically and constructively. Top and Tail in particular is a technique you could

use quite quickly and informally whenever you use a video, to establish the habit of checking out a text's sources.

Techniques 6, 7 and 8, **Generic Translations**, **Cross-media Comparisons** and **Simulation**, offer you more substantial classroom activities to explore ways of making changes to moving image texts and relating them to other media. In subject-specific contexts these can thus form the basis of coursework pieces at Key Stage 4, or could be used to set up class projects to explore an issue or topic.

Each technique is set out across three columns. The first column describes the activity itself and the second column provides some simple questions, which should help you to start the ball rolling in setting work or guiding whole-class discussion. Learning objectives are listed in the third column. These are moving-image specific, but if you accept our argument that 'cineliteracy' supports any subject, then you should find these useful insights that will contribute to communication and understanding in your subject area. We have avoided media jargon as much as possible, but the techniques necessarily introduce some simple and useful technical terms, most of which are explained in Unit 1.

interpa

BASIC TEACHING TECHNIQUE	KEY QUESTIONS	LEARNING OBJECTIVES
Freeze Frame Use the video pause button to help the class discuss each shot of a short moving image text or extract (eg 60 seconds long) by looking at and discussing: What they can see in the 'frozen' image; how the elements of the image are positioned in the frame; how lighting and colour affect what is seen. Distance between camera and subjects; camera angle; movement of the camera during a shot. How many shots there are and how the sequence of shots builds up information and ideas or impressions. *Possible follow-up:* Use a storyboard or moving image software to change the order of the sequence or eliminate some shots.	■ Why is the shot composed like this? What difference would it make if it were composed differently? ■ Why is the camera positioned in this way? What difference would it make if it were somewhere else? ■ What difference does it make if the order of shots is different or some are missing?	*Pupils should learn that:* ■ Every element of a visual image can carry meaning. ■ Visual images can be 'read' like other texts ■ The position of elements within the image, the colours used, and the lighting, can all affect interpretation. ■ Camera distance (eg close-up, long shot etc), camera angle and camera movement all affect meaning. ■ The number and order of shots affect meaning.
Sound and Image Cover the video screen and ask pupils to listen carefully to the soundtrack of a short moving image sequence and describe exactly what they hear in this sequence. Pupils should identify the type of text they think it is and identify and describe all the sounds they can hear. They should then guess at the content and style of the images in the sequence. Finally show the complete sequence and invite discussion about how sounds and images affect each other. *Possible follow-up* Try out any or all of: different music, different sound effects, a different voice reading the same words, or different words; or eliminate any of these elements. Discuss how this affects the ways the images can be interpreted.	*About music:* What kind of music is this? What feelings/images does it suggest to you? *About sound effects:* What exactly can you hear and what might it represent? *About words:* What is said and what can you tell about the speaker(s) from their voice(s)? *About silence:* Why do you think the sequence is silent at this point? What might be going on? *About the final viewing:* What difference does the sound make to the sequence? What difference would it make if some elements were missing?	■ Moving image sound tracks can have four elements: music, sound effects, voice and silence. All of these contribute to meaning. ■ Sound effects are of two types: 'atmosphere' (ie continuous sound) and 'spot effects' (ie short sounds). ■ Sound – particularly music – can set the 'mood' of a text and establish its generic identity (eg comedy, thriller). ■ Sound can often do more to 'pin down' the meaning of a sequence than visual images can. ■ Sound can affect not only the way viewers interpret the images but also what they actually think they can see. ■ Off-screen sounds can help to create the impression of three-dimensional space. ■ Silence can also have a powerful effect on the interpretation of a sequence.

BASIC TEACHING TECHNIQUE	KEY QUESTIONS	LEARNING OBJECTIVES

Spot the Shots

- After their first viewing of a short moving image sequence, pupils guess at the number of shots used.
- On second viewing, they mark each change in shot, scene location and sound (use pause button if necessary).
- On third viewing they look carefully at how the shot transitions are created (eg cuts, mixes, fades, wipes etc) and whether the sound transitions happen at the same places.
- They should also time each shot.

Possible follow-up:

- Create a script or storyboard to support their analysis of the sequence. Variations on the sequence can then be hypothesised: eg eliminating shots or changing the order of the sequence.
- If the software is available, pupils could digitize and re-edit the shots to try out different sequencing and timings.

Top and Tail

Show the title sequence of any moving image text and use any of Basic Techniques 1 to 3 to help pupils identify its genre and intended audience, and to predict its content and 'message'.
Show the production credits at the beginning and/or end of a moving image text and discuss the information they provide about the source and ownership of the text, how it was produced, and how it was distributed to audiences.

KEY QUESTIONS

- How long is this sequence? How much 'story time' does it represent?
- What new information or impression is each new shot giving us?
- What information or impression does each change in sound give us?
- Why is this kind of shot transition used? What difference would it make if another type of transition were used?
- Why are the shots of this length? Does the overall time-scheme of the shots build up a rhythm or a pattern? What is the effect of this?

- Is this a cinema film or a TV programme?
- Is it fact or fiction?
- Who is it for?
- What is it about?
- Who made it?
- Who owns it?
- Why might it have been made?
- What roles were involved in making it?

And how can you tell?

LEARNING OBJECTIVES

Pupils should learn that:

- The number, sequence and duration of shots in a moving image sequence all contribute to its meaning and are created in the editing process.
- Screen time and 'story time' are usually different: the editing process 'manages' the story time for us.
- Each new shot should provide new information or impressions: shot changes are not merely 'to keep viewer interest'.
- The pace and rhythm of editing and the types of transition used also contribute to meaning.
- Sound transitions may not match shot transitions: in drama especially they may anticipate them and this can function to maintain or develop moods such as suspense.
- Certain kinds of shot sequence are highly conventional: eg shot/reverse shot in a conversation or interview; or a character looking off-screen is likely to be followed by a shot of what they are looking at.

- Title sequences identify the text and 'sell' it to audiences; they may be very explicit about the text's genre, content, audience and purpose or they may disguise this to provoke curiosity.
- Information about who made a text, who financed it, and who owns it, can alert you to the interests it represents – and those it may not represent, or may misrepresent.
- Many roles may contribute to the production of a moving image text and can affect its content, style and meaning.
- A moving image text is likely to be produced by one company and distributed by another.

BASIC TEACHING TECHNIQUE	KEY QUESTIONS	LEARNING OBJECTIVES
Attracting Audiences ■ In pairs or groups, pupils collect information about how a text has been marketed and circulated to audiences: eg TV listings, educational resource catalogues, video catalogues, shop displays, websites, film posters, advertisements, trailers, TV ratings, cinema box office information, reviews, press releases, news items. Groups or pairs present their findings (eg as live presentations, poster montages etc) to the rest of the class, identifying key issues affecting the success or failure of a text to find its audience and convey its message.	■ What methods were used to promote this text to audiences? ■ Why were these methods used and not others? ■ Who helped promote this text and why? ■ Did audiences respond as the producers intended? If not, why not? ■ Was media controversy deliberately fostered? Did it help or harm the text? How?	*Pupils should learn that:* ■ Most moving image texts compete for audiences in a busy commercial market. ■ Moving image texts can be promoted in many different media. ■ Marketing and promotional strategies are central to most of the moving image industries. ■ Most media producers and distributors are part of larger conglomerates and can call upon a range of different companies to help promote their products. ■ Audience responses are measured and fed back into future production and promotion strategies. ■ Most moving image production and distribution is expensive and risky.
Generic Translation ■ Pupils 'translate' a moving image text – eg documentary, TV news item, TV or film commercial, scene from a feature film – into a print genre such as a newspaper item, a magazine feature, an extract from a novel, a short story or a poem. ■ Pupils translate a print text into moving image form – first as script or storyboard, and then if possible as video (a brief extract or 'try-out' of one scene).	■ What can you tell in print that you cannot tell or show in moving images? ■ What can you tell or show in moving images that you cannot tell in print? ■ Which medium do you think is best for the story/information/ideas you are conveying? ■ Is a real 'translation' ever possible from one medium to another?	■ Meaning can change when information is presented in different forms or transposed to another medium. ■ Each medium has its own language, conventions and genres. ■ Moving image is more appropriate for some kinds of content or structure, and print is more appropriate for others.

BASIC TEACHING TECHNIQUE	KEY QUESTIONS	LEARNING OBJECTIVES
Cross-media Comparisons Pupils can use Basic Techniques 1-6 to: ■ Compare the treatment of an issue in two different media and/or for two different audiences. ■ Compare a key moment from a fictional print text in two different moving image adaptations. ■ Compare treatments of the same theme in factual and fictional forms.	■ What elements stay the same and what changes (and how?) for the different audiences? ■ How do print and moving image respectively manage 'literary' features such as time, character, setting, motivation etc? ■ What is gained and what is lost in each form?	*Pupils should learn that:* ■ Groups, issues, values or ideas will be represented in different ways according to the form, genre and intended audience. ■ Print texts are open to a range of moving image adaptations. ■ Both documentary and drama can present a theme effectively; the boundary between fact and fiction can be hard to draw.
Simulation Pairs or groups of pupils are placed in role as producers of an existing moving image text used in any subject curriculum and asked to produce plans for how they would modify or reconstruct it for a different age-group; ■ 'sell' the text to a different audience; ■ challenge it critically from a particular point of view; ■ produce an alternative text. The plans should be presented to the teacher or another group acting as Commissioning Editor or Executive Producer.	■ Why have you chosen this age-group/audience? ■ What in the existing text will not appeal to, or be understood, by its new audience? ■ What aspects of the text can you use to sell it to its new audience? ■ What methods would be most appropriate to reach that audience? ■ From what point of view are you arguing against the text or for a different version? ■ What evidence are you using to back up your argument? ■ Who is the audience for the new version?	■ Most moving image texts are produced within editorial and institutional constraints: time, budget, context, purpose etc. ■ Content and form will vary according to audience and purpose. ■ Addressing a different audience can add ethical or legal factors which will affect what can and cannot be said or shown. ■ A critical challenge to an existing text must have good evidence to back it up which can come from both within the text itself and from other sources. ■ Alternatives are possible.

GENRE AND REPRESENTATION

Teaching Notes

The concept of representation faces any English teacher with a challenge. When you move with your students from analysing a written, or even a 'performed', literary text to an audio-visual text, you are forced to come to terms with the implications of the technology of cinema. Students are well aware from their earliest contact with storytelling that narratives offer a means of 're-presenting' events and emotional experiences. They learn to read a wide variety of stories, poems and plays and in each case come to recognise that there are conventions for presenting a story. They learn to harness their imagination in the service of interpreting different texts. But presented with a filmic narrative, many students will initially struggle to come to terms with the implications of photo-realistic imagery – their imagination is challenged in a new way.

What audiences see in much of mainstream cinema is designed to replicate the real and to place them in the position of spectator, which is self-effacing – effectively denying the process of watching and reading. Media theorists refer to this as a transparency effect.

The study of representations is concerned with exposing the constructed-ness of the filmic image (in terms of both sound and picture), helping students to understand that all film images are constructed, even those which appear to be showing the real world as it is. This is important, not least because cinema is a powerful tool for the promotion of ideas and emotions. However it is equally important to avoid classifying some images as negative because of

the ideas they promote, as this can lead to what has become known as the 'inoculation' approach to media education, which is based on the assumption that children and young people need to be protected from pernicious media texts. There is little evidence that this approach is effective in its own terms and, in any case, it is rather patronising in its suggestion that audiences are incapable of making

TO KILL A MOCKINGBIRD

individual readings. By providing the tools to enable readers to deconstruct images, media education aims to develop a critical awareness of the process of representation.

Representation study in film and television can be explored through five basic questions, which can be asked of any film text:

■ How close to reality is the world of the film meant to be? This is an aesthetic question about 'realism' and the way the world is represented to us.

■ How are familiar 'types' used in the film as a form of short-hand to represent people? What kinds of ideas of what is 'typical' does the film entertain? Who or what is representative?

■ Who is in control of the representations in the film – whose values and ideas are expressed in the film? (The writer or director may have particular views on the

issues in the film. The producers may be concerned to reflect mainstream opinion.)

■ What likelihood is there that different audiences will make different readings?

■ To what extent are the representations in the film related to changes in the 'real world' context of the film's production?

In the case studies we will touch upon aspects of all five of these questions (although we don't necessarily spell out all the questions for students).

KES

GENRE

The concept of genre as a critical tool has been central to the development of Film and Media Studies. It could be argued that the embracing of genre was one of the ways in which Media Studies distinguished itself from literary studies. For Media Studies, genre texts are interesting for the very reason that they have been neglected within English Literature – because of the patterns of repetition and difference that they display and because they function as texts through the manipulation of conventional features, now often referred to as the 'repertoire of elements', on which they draw. An established cinematic genre, such as the gangster film, can have a history of seventy years or more. In that time the elements of the genre have increased and combined and re-combined in many different ways.

Studying a genre's development over time allows us to question how the representation of the gangster (and of the police, city authorities etc) has changed and how it is related to changes in political, economic and social contexts. For instance, we might note the emergence of female gangsters/criminals (Bonnie Parker, Boxcar Bertha, Bloody Mama etc) in films in the late 1960s and early 1970s. This could be the result of film producers 'cashing in' on a big success (*Bonnie and Clyde*, 1967) and beginning a 'cycle' of similar films. But we also have to consider whether the cycle was sustained partly by the rise of the women's liberation movement in America at this time, and a desire by young audiences to see female characters like this on screen. Twenty-five years later, other genres, such as teen horror and action

adventure, are again representing young women as action heroes – a development which again is attracting academic interest.

For this pack, as for *Reading Films*, we have selected films that make use of a repertoire of elements that inform what are sometimes called 'youth pictures' or 'teen pictures'. The social context for this genre is clearly defined in historical terms by the emergence of 'teenagers' as a new consumer group in America in the early 1950s. There are also other ways to group the films and students should recognise that the value of genre study comes from what can be learned from grouping, re-grouping and studying similar characteristics in films rather than in any form of absolute definition.

THE YOUTH PICTURE

Some films can be grouped according to their 'target audience'. Youth pictures are targeted directly at audiences very roughly between the ages of 13 and 23 (in practice the target for each film may be even narrower). This doesn't mean that other audiences wouldn't also enjoy these films, but that in terms of representations, the films will deal with the 'youth world' and the leading characters will be within that age range. Crucially, also, the themes of the films will be those associated with adolescence – adults generally will be 'them' rather than 'us'.

Pleasantville and *Buffy* are clearly youth pictures (as well as 'fantasy' films and comedies). They are set in high schools/small town

bfi British Film Institute

communities and deal with adolescent problems, although these are played out in a context much wider than just the school or community. *Kes* shares many features with these two, but it would not usually be seen as a youth picture, despite drawing on the same elements – school/community, young central character, themes of growing up etc. Instead, *Kes* is most likely to be seen as a 'social realist drama'. Its target audience is more universal and audiences are expected to 'read' the film via its appeal to realism and social issues rather than to the familiar generic conventions of the American high school comedy. This doesn't mean, of course, that students couldn't approach *Kes* in the same way,

but the film industry and film critics would tend to group *Kes* with *To Kill a Mockingbird*, as they share a sense of the importance of setting and a major social issue rather than the theme of young people 'discovering' things about life and themselves. (Both films were directed by filmmakers with strong 'artistic' reputations – Ken Loach for politics and realism, Robert Mulligan for sensitive stories about children.) *Kes* and *To Kill a Mockingbird* might also be linked through the process of close and 'faithful' adaptation of a literary text.

The Wizard of Oz was made before the concept of the youth picture was developed. However, its star, Judy Garland, was one of the forerunners of modern youth stars and it would

be possible to argue that in the film the 13-year-old Dorothy is involved in a 'teen adventure'. (*The Wizard of Oz* is a 'road movie' as well as a fantasy and a musical.)

The only film selected here that does not draw on the youth picture repertoire is *The Crucible*. We have linked it to *Pleasantville* because of its allegorical features – it could also be linked in formal terms to the two literary adaptations.

Students are likely to be familiar with the concept of genre, partly because of their own familiarity with the way in which media industries distribute their products, partly because the term itself is increasingly used by stars talking about their film roles etc. Although the term and the concept are quite well-known, there is little understanding of why genre is a useful critical tool. We want students to see that genre ideas help us to 'open up' films for analysis. Through looking for patterns of 'repetition and difference', including the mixing together of elements from different genres, we can reveal some of the intricate ways in which films represent people and places, ideas and emotions. In Unit 2 we extend this to consider how genre helps to construct allegories and metaphors.

In this unit the Student Notes mainly discuss films in general terms. However, Activity 3 uses specific schoolroom scenes from *Kes* and *Buffy* or *Pleasantville*. These scenes should be selected and lined up before the lesson.

THE CRUCIBLE

Unit 1

GENRE AND REPRESENTATION

— + Student Notes & Activities + —

THE WIZARD OF OZ

In this course on moving image media texts you will be asked to think about films and television programmes in a particular way. Most of the time, when you watch a film you expect to be entertained. Sometimes, especially with certain television programmes you expect to be informed about a particular subject. But all the time you are watching you are also experiencing something else – you are recognising and remembering certain things about the way in which the film tells its story, how characters are presented, what kinds of ideas, values and emotions the film is interested in. Sometimes a film comes along that seems a little bit different and this gets everyone talking about these broader issues. In recent films, such as *Charlie's Angels* (US, 2000), *Lara Croft: Tomb Raider* (US/UK, 2001) and *The Mummy Returns* (US, 2001), we have seen young women as action heroes, and the experience of watching women in these roles may be more important to some audiences than the outcome of the story.

The knowledge you gain from watching a wide range of films over several years is important in developing two sets of critical tools that you can use to study any film. The first of these refers to **genre**.

GENRE

This French word refers to a category or a specific group of films. 'Genre study' suggests that we can group films together that have similar characteristics or 'elements'. We might for instance, look out for films that share:

- characters
- settings (location, period in history etc)
- stories
- use of music and sound effects
- use of camera or special effects (style).

The first three elements in this list are relevant to both film study and literature study, but the last two are important solely for film. Sometimes it only takes a few minutes to recognise the 'look' and 'sound' of a film and to identify particular genres as being relevant.

Most films include 'elements' taken from more than one genre and mixed together. In this course we are mostly dealing with films that could be described as 'youth pictures'. But these films also include elements of 'comedy', 'horror' and 'social drama'.

Youth pictures

These are films made for audiences aged (very roughly) 13 to 23, so this is a genre defined first by its audience. In practice, film classifications identify some 'youth pictures' as suitable only for over 15s and over 18s. Young people in this age range go to the cinema more frequently than anyone else, so filmmakers are keen to attract this target audience by using stories that focus on youth figures as central characters. What other elements might be included?

- Other characters – in most youth pictures, the story will involve some kind of conflict with authority, represented by teachers, parents, the police, the military etc;
- Settings – school/college, streets/clubs/bars, training camp etc;
- Stories – romance, academic or sporting success, 'proving yourself';
- Popular music, chart music, dance music etc used throughout;
- Fast editing, lively and colourful look.

1 In groups, select any recent film that you think might be a youth picture (or a 'teen' picture, as Hollywood sometimes describes them).
- **Try to identify the five elements above (character, settings, stories, music and style) in this film. Are they all relevant?**

THE CRUCIBLE

- **Are there other elements that you think are important in a youth picture?**
- **If there are enough different choices between groups, you can pool all your findings as a class and decide whether you think there is enough evidence to justify defining the youth picture genre.**

Don't worry if your discussion is not conclusive. Our aim is not to identify every film as belonging to a specific genre. What is more important is that discussing the elements in a film in a systematic way opens up a film for study. It helps us to ask some useful questions and often, through comparisons with similar films, to discover things about the film that we might not have noticed before. What a genre study reveals is a pattern of 'repetition and difference'. Sometimes you hear critics suggesting that a film has been made to a formula, that it is using the same mix of elements each time. If this were the case, films would be very boring. There will be the repetition of some elements, but others will have changed to produce a new and different mix. Over several years, the mix of elements in a genre can change quite noticeably. Youth pictures seem to change more than other genres.

BUFFY THE VAMPIRE SLAYER

2 Watch any film with young central characters (on television or video) that is more than ten years old. What are the obvious differences in what the characters do or how they are shown, compared to a modern youth picture?

MIXING GENRES

Most films mix elements from more than one genre. Comedy elements are used extensively in all kinds of films. The 'teen comedy' has been very popular in recent years. For example, the television series *Buffy the Vampire Slayer* combines elements of the youth picture with both comedy and horror. Again, horror is a popular genre with the youth audience. The 1960s film *Kes* (UK, 1969), which you may focus on in this course, uses some of the elements of the youth picture, but overall it tries to be a very different kind of film, concentrating on presenting its story as being 'real' and uncompromising. Interestingly, *Kes* looks and sounds different to most youth pictures.

PLEASANTVILLE

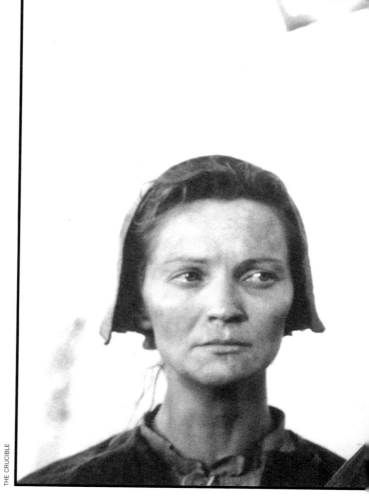
THE CRUCIBLE

This doesn't mean genre is not a useful tool in studying *Kes* – what is different or missing is often as important as what is there.

3 Look at the ways in which websites, shops, magazines and reference guides describe films.
■ If you have internet access, log on to the Internet Movie Database at http://uk.imdb.com and check out some well-known films. How does the IMDB describe them? Which genres does it list for each film? Are most films listed as 'mixes'?
■ How does your local video shop classify films for rent? If it just displays them alphabetically, check on the box how the distributor describes them. Do you agree with the descriptions of films you know?

■ You could also look in your local library and see if any of the novels are placed on separate shelves for 'genre fiction'. The library probably puts only a small proportion of novels on shelves marked 'Westerns', 'Science Fiction', 'Romance' or 'Crime'. This is the opposite of films where most films are given some form of classification. Why do you think this is?

Recognising genres is not usually very difficult (and anyway there isn't a 'right answer' as such). Once you are clear about what we mean by genre, the real challenge is to use 'genre knowledge' in your film analysis.

TO KILL A MOCKINGBIRD

REPRESENTATION

This is another key concept or critical tool for studying film, which you will already have come across in English Literature. In film study it assumes a special importance because of all the extra ways in which films can create meanings through use of camerawork, lighting, editing etc, as well as through using well-known stars to play particular roles.

The illusion of reality

The first and most important idea associated with representation is that everything we see and hear on the cinema screen has been created or constructed for our viewing and listening. This sounds obvious, but if you think about how you watch films you will realise that film has certain qualities that make us forget that it is all an illusion. For a start, film consists of a sequence of still images (frames on a filmstrip) projected onto a screen at the rate of 24 frames per second – ie so quickly that they appear to move.

Film is essentially a realist medium. We see a couple driving along a Los Angeles freeway or getting on a London bus and we believe this is really happening. Unlike a novel or even a play, we are not asked to imagine the scene: it is presented to us as it would be in 'real life'. Not only that, we are offered different views of the scene – we can get on the bus with the couple, and sit down next to them. Camerawork and editing have been developed to help us forget that we are watching a film. The techniques the filmmaker uses have become 'invisible' or 'transparent' – we ignore them and just follow the story. Nearly every Hollywood-style film has this quality, but there are other aspects of film that work in different ways.

KES

PLEASANTVILLE

We may follow the story of the couple on the bus, happily forgetting that this is a 'made-up' story, but how do we account for the music on the soundtrack or the dramatic lighting that signals the spectacular crash which awaits our heroes in a few moments? Again, we are willing to 'suspend our disbelief' and go along with the story. We accept that the film is offering us experience of a coherent fictional world in which this story happens. That world draws on our experience of the 'real world' and re-presents it to us. There are many different ways to do this and the first representation question we want to ask of any film is – How close does a film claim to be to the 'real world'?

4 **Look at a few minutes from a school scene in *Kes* and in *Pleasantville* (US, 1998) or *Buffy the Vampire Slayer*.**

Compare the look and sound of the film and the behaviour of the characters. How are they different? Which feels more like a real school? Why?

Audience identification

The second important issue that connects any film with the 'real world' concerns our own sense of identity and the way in which we engage with characters on the screen. We all watch films slightly differently, but most of us 'identify' with one or more of the central characters, hoping they will 'succeed' in the story. This also means we hope that the 'villain' will fail. In a novel, the main characters are described in detail, and in our imaginations they can seem very like us. But on the screen the 'hero' is often played by a well-known

THE WIZARD OF OZ

TO KILL A MOCKINGBIRD

A film lasts around two hours. We have only a short time in which to get to know the characters, understand their motivations, needs and desires and follow the action. As a result, filmmakers have to find ways of presenting characters to us in 'shorthand'. This is known as 'typing' – instead of each character being a very complex human being who would take hours to understand, we are presented with a 'typical' character who we recognise quite quickly and feel confident that we understand. There are three different kinds of character typing:

- An **archetype** is a familiar character who has emerged from hundreds of years of storytelling, including myths, legends, folktales and fairy tales.
- A **stereotype** is a character description based on more modern classifications used initially by marketing and social surveys. Stereotypes are often defined by age, social class, ethnic group, etc. While stereotypes are sometimes used in films, they are more usually referred to in news stories. Often this is a 'negative' typing of, eg, 'teenage mothers' or 'asylum seekers'.
- A **generic type** is a character familiar from repetitive use in a particular genre. For example, we have learned that in a gangster genre there is often a group of not very bright hoodlums, a cold and efficient assassin, a corrupt lawyer or accountant etc.

5 If you were asked to set up a scene for a high school movie showing a typical class, what kind of characters would you create to quickly clue the audience into the actions they can associate with individual characters? (You could look at the openings of films like *Clueless* (US, 1995) or *Ten Things I Hate About You* (US, 1999) to get some ideas.)

6 The classroom in *Kes* is presented in a much more 'realistic' way than in the American films. Can you still find recognisable 'types' in the school in *Kes*? If you can, are they the same types represented by films set in American high schools?

The use of 'types' is a feature of most films, even if it is more obvious in some cases than others. Just as most films display genre elements of some kind, most characters deploy some form of typing. In some cases the character type has one specific role to play in the text. However, the character types of main characters may be filled out and shown to have special individual qualities as the story line of the film is developed.

actor who is handsome or beautiful, witty and accomplished, and adored by the opposite sex. Are they like us? Would they even give us the time of day in the street? The character may be played by a star we've seen on a TV chat show or read about in a magazine. Film stars have to combine two completely contradictory qualities in order to be successful. They must be 'special' (sexually attractive, beautiful, strong, clever, etc) and they must be plausible as the 'boy or girl next door'. It's a tall order, but they must act as the 'representative' of the audience in the cinema if most of us are to become involved in the story. Our next representation questions are therefore –

What kinds of characters appear in the film?

Which groups in society are represented and what does the film seem to be saying about them?

Unit 2
SOCIAL CONTEXT, METAPHOR AND ALLEGORY
Teaching Notes

KES

This unit aims to introduce students to ways of thinking about films which may be unfamiliar to them. It explores the concept of metaphor and allegory in an audiovisual medium and it stresses the idea that films are made within a specific production context and then distributed and 'read' by audiences in a specific 'reception' context. Although the unit requires the skills of textual analysis developed in Unit 1, it also aims to involve students in thinking about the importance of film texts as a focus for attention on a series of wider social issues.

In selecting the six films for case studies, we have chosen three films that all in some way engage with major social issues in 1950s' America:

- **The Crucible** presents the trial of the Salem witches in the seventeenth century as a means of raising questions about the political hysteria of the McCarthy era (and subsequent similar periods of irrational social behaviour).
- **Pleasantville** attempts to explore both the repressive tendencies of

McCarthyism and the call for Civil Rights in the context of conservative white America of the 1950s.
- **To Kill a Mockingbird**, although set in the 1930s, was produced in 1962 and was clearly seen as a contribution to the debate about Civil Rights.

We have provided some background information about America in the 1950s and you may feel that an integrated project looking at literature and writing about this period would give a strong focus for students' work.

The other three films present allegories about rather broader issues. All are in some way about 'growing up' – *Kes* in the Britain of the 1960s, and *Buffy the Vampire Slayer* in contemporary America (and *Pleasantville* also addresses this). *The Wizard of Oz* has perhaps the most 'universal' theme and the allegory, which centres on American politics in the 1890s, is deeply buried for most audiences, even if the moral values are easily recognised.

The six films can also be grouped in two other ways which are both concerned with the potential differences between film and literature as allegorical forms. *To Kill a Mockingbird*, *Kes*, *The Crucible* and *The Wizard of Oz* are all literary adaptations. The first three are faithful adaptations that have been presented to audiences as having serious artistic and social merits. Part of this is to do with the artistic claims of the relevant directors, stars etc, and part to do with the aesthetics adopted by the films. Because of this, there has been little difficulty in persuading educators that these are worthwhile texts. *Kes* and *To Kill a Mockingbird* are two of the most studied modern literary texts in the UK and US respectively. Whether this status is something that students recognise is perhaps worth exploring – students will clearly see that these are films that are different from those they usually see at the multiplex. Will they also think that such films are supposed to be 'good for them'?

This status for *Mockingbird*, *Kes* and *The Crucible* becomes more interesting if any one of the three is compared to *Pleasantville*, *Buffy* or *The Wizard of Oz*. These films are more clearly part of popular culture and are most likely to have been received as genre films. The 'teen' genre, along with the musical and the children's film, is generally not considered to have serious artistic merit. All three are, in these terms, unlikely sources for allegory and metaphor. Again this is something worth exploring with students. *Buffy*, in particular, may raise some interesting questions. Although its

slots on UK television (BBC2 tea-time and late night, and Sky One) mean that it is outside the mainstream, the show has a devoted army of fans, not all of whom are teenagers. It has also attracted a great deal of academic interest from film, media and cultural studies.

Pleasantville, *Buffy* and *The Wizard of Oz* are also marked by their reliance on obvious artifice to create a fantasy world. Quality drama in

TO KILL A MOCKINGBIRD

the UK traditionally relies heavily upon realist codes – expressed through authentic costumes and sets, music, dialogue, etc – and the maintenance of an illusion of transparent narrative development (ie not drawing attention to the telling of the story). Films that do not conform to this aesthetic may be popular box office winners but may fail to find critical acceptance. We think that this is a false and not very helpful distinction and one aim of the pack is to present both kinds of film as the potential bases for metaphor and allegory.

USING THE CASE STUDY MATERIAL

Above we suggest that there is an aesthetic division between two groups of films, but there is also a thematic /generic division with *Pleasantville*, *Mockingbird* and *The Crucible* referring directly to social and political issues in American society whereas *Kes*, *Buffy* and *The Wizard of Oz* refer to the problems of growing up. It is also possible to use *Pleasantville* in relation to these ideas and to look at *Kes* and *The Wizard of Oz* in terms of what they say about social issues and politics.

There are many options for grouping the films, but we have included a greater number of activities for *Pleasantville*, *The Crucible* and *Kes*. We've used the films as examples in the two sets of Student Notes for this unit (but the notes still make sense, even if students don't see all the films). If your time is limited, you should screen one of these three films before the students start work on Unit 2 and select a second film to screen as a Case Study (ie undertake two case studies). You can select a pairing that will emphasise the aesthetic differences as well as the way in which similar, or at least linked, metaphors are explored. For example:

- *Pleasantville* with *The Crucible* or *To Kill a Mockingbird*;
- *Kes* with *Buffy* or *The Wizard of Oz*;
- *The Crucible* with *Pleasantville* etc.

In each case, you should find that there are some surprising parallels, although on the surface the texts are very different. *Buffy* may treat high school in what seems like a light-hearted way, but some of its genre elements are shared with *Kes* (eg the importance of a teacher (a non-parent adult figure), the single parent or dysfunctional family background, the isolated figure in the classroom). If students can engage with both 'realist' and 'fantasy' texts in their analysis, they will develop a much deeper understanding of the way in which film texts produce meaning and the way in which audiences can engage with such meanings.

Unit 2A
THE SOCIAL CONTEXT OF FILM PRODUCTION
+ Student Notes & Activities +

THE WIZARD OF OZ

Watching a film is quite a different experience to reading a book. Think about the ways in which these experiences differ.

1 In small groups make two lists, one of films you have watched, and another of books or short stories you have read, during the past few weeks. What are the most noticeable differences between your two lists? Share your findings with the rest of the class.

You should immediately become aware of the different ways we receive films and books. A book is rarely read in one sitting and it can take months to finish, whereas a film is usually viewed all the way through at once. Indeed, it can be very frustrating to have to leave a film before the end and our enjoyment is affected if this happens. A book, on the other hand, can be fully enjoyed when reading only a few chapters at a time.

2 Again in your groups, make a list of the factors that help you to decide which film you want to see.

You could have a favourite actor, or director. You may prefer films of a particular genre, for example, Science Fiction or Horror. You might have read a review that sounds interesting in a national newspaper or film magazine. Your friends may be raving about a new release.

3 Go back to your list of films. What seem to be the most popular kinds of film in your particular group?

Obviously your likes and dislikes are important in terms of the kinds of films that are produced by the film industry. Any film will need to attract a large audience and make money. In Hollywood today, popular story sources for films include: adaptations from best-selling books; plays or classic novels; comic strips or video games; modern versions of fairytales; major historical events; and original stories from well-known scriptwriters.

When we think about the ways in which a film is produced and received in our society, it is important to consider the pleasure it gives us and the meanings that it conveys.

4 In small groups or as a whole class conduct a small survey of film-watching habits.

- Decide on a number of questions that you can ask members of your family or friends. Aim to find out how often they watch films; how often they go to the cinema; whether they have a favourite cinema and why; and what makes them want to see a particular kind of film.
- Each member of the group should be responsible for getting answers to the chosen questions.
- When the various surveys have been completed, analyse the information you have received and report back to the whole class.
- You will probably find that there are a number of differences in viewing habits. Try to work out whether social factors, like age, gender or community, make a difference.

The way we receive films and their meanings will depend on a variety of social factors. They can also change over time. Arthur Miller adapted *The Crucible* for the cinema in 1996, he originally wrote the play in 1953. As a playwright, you may think he would prefer the medium of drama to convey his ideas. However, when working on his adaptation he said,

> 'The film, by reaching the broad American audience as no play ever can, may well unearth still other connections to those buried public terrors that Salem announced on this continent'.

5 Take a few moments to think about this quotation. What according to Miller is the important advantage that film holds over drama in today's society? What might he be saying about changes in the meanings we receive from *The Crucible*?

6 In small groups brainstorm the number of films that you have seen that were originally plays or novels. Pick one of these adaptations. What are the main differences between the book/play and the film?

7 You may have seen Baz Luhrmann's film *William Shakespeare's Romeo and Juliet* (US, 1996). You may also have seen or read Shakespeare's play.

- What are the most striking differences between the film world created by Baz Luhrmann and that of the play?
- How successful do you think the film was?
- Were you able to make connections with modern social issues/problems more easily because the play had been adapted in such a modern way?

In this course we look at films that were either made with the intention of 'saying something about the world' or, in the case of *The Wizard of Oz*, made use of an original story that was written with such an intent. This doesn't mean that any of the films is particularly preachy or dull. All of the films have found appreciative audiences. The films all make a comment on social issues, but they do so in different ways and by comparing two films with the same concerns, but expressed very differently, we can learn how to analyse a film text. We also need to be aware at this point that whenever a film is set (eg *The Crucible* is set in the seventeenth century) it is usually in some way commenting on 'now' – the time when it is being produced. There is also another 'now' – the time when we are 'reading' the film and trying to make sense of it. Readers are important – we can interpret films in new ways that involve our understanding of both the world around us and the world as it was when the film was made.

The films in this course deal with historical events, or 'personal events' set in an historical period. Some background information about this period – the 1950s and 60s – may therefore be useful. The social issues discussed here are well-documented, so it is easy to research them in detail.

AMERICA IN THE 1950s

The United States became a world superpower after the Second World War. Before the war, the US was the biggest economic power, but the pre-war governments concentrated on problems at home and tried not to get involved overseas. After the war, however, they became far more involved across the world in order, as they saw it, to stop the Soviet Union (Russia) spreading its influence.

Communism

The basic idea of communism – that everyone in a community should share ownership of everything, including land, businesses etc – is a philosophy with a long tradition. In the twentieth century it became almost solely associated with a particularly repressive form of government in the Soviet Union. In some countries, communist governments were elected; in others, communists took control after a violent revolution. The fear of communism was strongest in the United States, which had a long tradition of individualism and opposition to any form of collective ownership. In the United States in the 1950s a suspected communist was treated with the same distrust and hostility that a supporter of Al Qa'ida faces now.

PLEASANTVILLE

Living in the shadow of the bomb

The period known as the 'Cold War' lasted over forty years in which Russia and America saw each other as 'arch enemies' and built more and more nuclear weapons in order to 'defend' themselves against each other's perceived threat. Young people growing up in the 1950s lived with the fear of nuclear war. You could ask your parents or grandparents what it was like to live in fear of 'the bomb'. They were known first as A-bombs – 'atomic bombs', and then as H-bombs – hydrogen bombs. In Britain, both British and America weapons were installed to counteract a possible attack by the Soviet Union. Many people joined the CND (Campaign for Nuclear Disarmament) and its 'Ban the Bomb' movement. The threat of nuclear war became very real in 1962 when the Americans and the Russians played a game of brinkmanship, each pushing the other side to the brink of war – a war in which millions would have died and from which the whole world would have suffered possibly disastrous consequences. The Cuban missile crisis, which was at the centre of this war game, was eventually defused, but the Cold War lasted until the 1990s when the Soviet Union gradually broke up.

The paradox of 1950s' America

A paradox is a situation where two contradictory ideas exist at the same time. In America in the 1950s, the fear of the bomb and the pleasures of prosperity existed at the same time. The image of the ideal community was in fact a disguise for much nastier things happening underneath the surface. One of them was the racism that ran throughout American society. In reality, America was not very different from South Africa – black people did not have equality before the law and in the southern states there was racial segregation. During the 1950s black people began to stage protests which developed into the Civil Rights movement of the 1960s.

Most Americans had very little idea of what communism or socialism was and it was possible for some extremist politicians to stir up a 'witch-hunt' against anybody in America who might be a 'communist sympathiser'. During the 1930s a number of writers, actors and directors had joined the American Communist Party because they were disgusted with the levels of hardship and unemployment caused by the capitalist system during the Great Depression. Now they found themselves being hunted out and exposed by a political campaign led by Senator McCarthy. Hollywood became a focus of the witch-hunts against communists that characterised this campaign.

8 Try to imagine a society in which everyone is afraid of war – a war in which your strange next door neighbours could be helping the enemy. Brainstorm some ideas about stories that could be set in this context.

Unit 2B

METAPHOR AND ALLEGORY

┤Student Notes & Activities├

TO KILL A MOCKING BIRD

These notes deal with a group of 'story devices' – things that writers can do to develop specific meanings in all kinds of media texts such as novels, short stories, poems, songs, plays and films.

METAPHOR

'Metaphor' comes from the Greek and means 'to carry over'. In effect, meaning is 'carried over' from one object to another. In our study of representation in Unit 1 we learned that films have to find ways to 'represent' characters and their actions. A metaphor is a particular kind of representation in which what the filmmaker wants to say about a person, an idea or an event is represented by a very different image. The filmmaker hopes that the audience will be able to make the connection. This poses the question: Why make it seemingly more difficult for the audience?

It may not be difficult at all and, in fact, the metaphor may make it easier to understand the action and may also make more impact on the viewer. In the novel, *A Kestrel for a Knave*, the author Barry Hines describes Billy Casper's first sighting of a hawk:

'A speck appeared on the horizon, it held like a star, then fell and faded'.

This description uses a device called a **simile** – often introduced by using 'like'. This makes a simple connection between the kestrel hovering in the distance and a star as a bright speck in the night sky. A **metaphor** is an extension of such a connection so that the reader thinks about the representation of one thing and then relates it in quite complex ways to what it is connected to. So a metaphor doesn't just make the image more vivid, but also makes us think about what it means.

Think about the image of a shooting star in the night sky. It suddenly appears as a bright object in the sky, shoots across our vision and then dies away. It seems to have come from nowhere, blazed brightly and then disappeared. Have you noticed how this 'trajectory' of the shooting star has been applied to the careers of pop stars or movie stars? They suddenly appear in the limelight, everyone adores them, and then they 'burn out'. This extended metaphor has been used in countless films, even though we know that in real life 'stars' are not born overnight and that most of them gradually disappear from view. However, the metaphor of stardom makes for a better story.

1 Jot down any films you have seen that deal with the story of a star's rise to fame and glory. These are sometimes called 'biopics' and deal with stars from the worlds of music, film, sports etc.
- Can you point to anything in the films that suggests that the metaphor of 'stars in the sky' is being used to present 'stars in the media'?

- How might these ideas be used in a biopic about a star – 'the birth of a star', 'a galaxy of stars' 'shining bright', 'light-years away' 'burn-out'?
- Can you think of any other metaphors for the rise and fall of a star?

SYMBOLS

Another device that writers and filmmakers use is the symbol. A symbol is an image which has gradually acquired a range of meanings through repeated use over a long period of time. Symbols are often quite simple images that are easily remembered and recognised. This gives them enormous power and the meanings which they carry can be very highly-charged.

One of the most famous symbols across the world is the crucifix, the image of Christianity. Filmmakers have used this symbol in many different ways. In the 1958 film of *Dracula* (UK), the vampire is destroyed when Van Helsing creates a crucifix by holding two candlesticks at right angles. As the light streams through a window it creates a shadow of the crucifix across the vampire who crumbles to dust. Here is an excellent example of the power of the symbol.

Other common symbols include the dove as a symbol of peace. A film that starts with a hunter shooting a dove – by design or by accident – is likely to signal the start of a war or a conflict of some kind.

2 When might the following symbols be used in a film and for what purpose?
- a crown
- a swastika
- a man and a woman standing together 'arm in arm'.

There are many films that use symbols to represent ideas and actions in this way. Sometimes it is simply a matter of providing a 'shorthand' image; sometimes it makes the film more powerful in its impact on the audience. Sometimes the use of symbols is very complex and depends on the audience to work hard and have some additional knowledge about the symbol to understand its full meaning. You may see a film and think that a particular image is important but not understand why.

For example, in Spain between 1939 and 1975, the dictator General Franco imposed severe censorship on all films. Filmmakers were not allowed to criticise the church, the state,

PLEASANTVILLE

THE CRUCIBLE

tradition, etc. They had to find ways of being critical through using symbols in such a way that the authorities could not prove what the films meant. One film, *The Spirit of the Beehive* (Spain, 1973), makes extensive use of symbols, but unless you know a great deal about Spain and its history, the meaning is not clear. The title of the film refers to the practice of keeping bees. The bees work very hard to produce honey which the beekeeper must then steal from them. To keep them dozy when the honey is being taken, the beekeeper puffs smoke into the hive. While there is nothing very surprising or exciting about showing this, the filmmaker may be able make us see the connection between the bees and the Spanish population, between the beekeeper and the dictator who keeps the people 'dozy'. The beehive is a symbol of collective hard work (the 'busy bee'). Smoking the bees is a metaphor for keeping the population quiet. The whole film becomes an **allegory**, a story in which symbols are used extensively.

ALLEGORY

Allegory comes from the Greek for 'speak of other' and suggests that whatever a particular kind of story seems to be about, we should read it as referring to something else. The 'something else' can be understood by the use of symbols. An allegory can be read on two or more levels.

For example, Aesop's well-known fable or short story about the tortoise and the hare is a simple allegory comparing how people approach life and the consequences of different approaches. The tortoise represents the slow, meticulous and thoughtful person who eventually reaches her goal – the hare, on the other hand is full of self-conceit, impulsive and rash and fails to reach her goal.

An allegory is an extended metaphor in that we can read an entire story as standing for something else. Allegories allow powerful comments on contemporary problems during times when to openly criticise policies, systems or political figures may mean the artist would incur sanctions, or lay themselves open to personal attack. Throughout history whenever a society has been in turmoil, artists have looked for new ways to express themselves.

In English literature a number of famous plays, novels and poems have used a more complicated allegorical form in order to explore social issues. Arthur Miller's play *The Crucible* focuses upon real witch trials in Salem, Massachusetts in 1692. On a deeper, symbolic level the play deals with the American fear

KES

of communism in the early 1950s. Harper Lee's novel *To Kill a Mockingbird* was written in 1959 and refers to an incident in Alabama in the 1930s but it was taken by many readers to be a comment on events in the 1950s when the struggle for Civil Rights was beginning.

ALLEGORY IN FILMS

All films tell stories. Stories can be understood on different levels. In Unit 1 we learned that a film 'represents' the world and offers us a particular version of reality. On the surface a story is about a group of characters and what happens to them. On a deeper level, we may see the characters as representative in some way, so what happens to a special group of characters in a film may suggest what happens to everyone in a particular community, or everyone in America. At a deeper level still, we may read the film as an allegory – a story in which all events are symbolic, referring to something else in the real world. Titles and character names can carry symbolic meanings.

3 In *The Crucible* what kind of expectations of the story does the title offer us? Look the word up in a large dictionary. What meanings does it have, or is it linked to, and how do these influence your expectations of the play?

4 Similarly, 'Pleasantville' is a very suggestive name. What does it imply?

How are characters in stories named? Most of the time, names sound realistic or authentic – names we would expect in a particular community, such as in *The Godfather* (US, 1972), where the gangsters have Italian names. But sometimes the character's name tells us something about his or her qualities or role in the plot. This is especially so in an allegorical story. In George Orwell's *Animal Farm* – an allegory about the political ideas of the 1940s – the animals have carefully chosen names. One of the pigs who takes over the farm is called Napoleon (after the dictator Napoleon Bonaparte). The carthorse on the farm is called 'Boxer'. What kind of a character does the name 'Boxer' suggest and which group of people in society might be symbolised by Boxer, the carthorse?

Similarly in *The Crucible*, the couple who are the victims of the witch-hunt are the Proctors – a 'proctor' was an official in England, a representative of the clergy in the courts and an enforcer of regulations in the universities. This is an ironic choice of name in the context of the play.

Filmmakers have a big advantage when it comes to creating allegories. As well as all the devices available to the novelist they can call on music, colour, camerawork etc. Music and colour are sometimes powerful symbols – what do you feel when a national anthem like the Stars and Stripes is played in a film, or even just a style of orchestral music that suggests a national anthem? In the old Westerns the trumpet call and a particular kind of martial music usually signalled the arrival of the Fifth Cavalry – symbolic of American military power. This symbol is now tarnished because we recognise how brutally the Native Americans were treated.

Modern films have created new musical symbols to represent the American government. For example, the television series *The West Wing* opens with a dramatic music track featuring drums and full orchestra to accompany the aerial shots of the White House – the symbol of American democracy. Similar music is found in

THE CRUCIBLE

films that depict contemporary American military adventures. Colour can also be symbolic. There is still bitter conflict in Northern Ireland and it would be foolish to wear the Protestant Orange or the Catholic Green in the wrong location. In a very different context, director Baz Luhrmann has described his three films – *Strictly Ballroom* (Australia, 1992), *Romeo and Juliet* and *Moulin Rouge* (US/Australia, 2001) – as 'red curtain' films, referring to the curtain that opens to reveal the stage in a theatre, as it does in *Strictly Ballroom* at the start of the film. The red curtain symbolises not just the theatrical and artificial nature of the films but also their central concern with passion and emotion. *Pleasantville* (US 1998)makes excellent use of a particularly red apple and a red rose.

One other crucial factor for filmmakers is casting. A well-known star in a particular role can work in a symbolic way. As soon as Gregory Peck appeared on screen in *To Kill a Mockingbird* (US, 1962), audiences knew that he would not only a good and gentle father, but also the voice of 'liberal America'. Peck represented a Hollywood hero who would be thoughtful and sensitive. (Later this image was turned upside down very effectively when Peck played a terrifying Nazi doctor in film *The Boys from Brazil* (US, 1978).)

5 **You have been asked to make a film that is an allegory for life as a young person in Britain today. The film should attempt to comment on British society through the use of symbols to represent social attitudes etc. The central character is a young man or woman who goes on a journey around the country.**
■ **Who would you cast in the lead role?**

■ **How would they be dressed (what kind of haircut etc)?**
■ **What kinds of music would accompany them on their travels?**
■ **What kinds of people would they meet?**

The film, *The Crucible* (US, 1996), can be read as an allegory in its use of character, colour, music etc. The opening of a play, novel, or film is very important. It is here that we are usually introduced to the main characters, genre is established and the audience's attention is engaged. In a play or novel the spoken or written word usually carries the metaphorical and allegorical elements but in a film the visual imagery is an important way of 'carrying over' meaning.

6 **Watch the opening sequence (approx. four minutes) of *The Crucible*. Miller called the first act of his play 'An Overture'. Its function was to set a scene in which hysteria, fear, guilt and suspicion dominate. How do the following elements of the film language in the opening sequence combine to fulfil this function?**
■ **Music and sound**
■ **Lighting and colour**
■ **Setting props and costume.**
How do the title graphics combine with the background music to create atmosphere?

PLEASANTVILLE

Case Studies

PLEASANTVILLE

+ Student Notes & Activities +

Pleasantville (US, 1998) is a film that can be 'read' on different levels. David and Jennifer have an adventure and we are interested in how they react to their new situation. They are transported into a fantasy world – the world of David's favourite 1950s TV sitcom. (For more information on the typical 1950s' American sitcom see the end of this Case Study.) They begin the film as ordinary teenagers in 1990s' America and show us something about American youth culture through what they say and do.

1 Watch the opening sequence of *Pleasantville* (up to when the teenagers' mother leaves for the weekend).
- **What issues are raised about the way young people live and relate to each other in 1990s' America?**
- **Are all the values represented as positive?**
- **What problems are raised in this sequence?**

Although *Pleasantville* has many of the characteristic elements of a fairy tale or fantasy, it is also an imaginative, original tale that poses interesting questions about contemporary society. On the one hand, it's a fantasy in which two late-twentieth-century teenagers are transported into a black-and-white Utopia (an imagined perfect place or state of things). On the other hand, it works on the levels of metaphor and allegory, commenting on social and philosophical issues. Gary Ross, the writer and director of the film, stated that his initial idea was to ask,

'What would happen if there was a place where there was no colour, noise, doubt or uncertainty? What if a world like a 1950s' sitcom, where everyone is polite and predictable, came to life?'

2 **In groups, draw up a brief outline of what a perfect society might be like.**
- **What would you like to eliminate in order to create a perfect world?**
- **What is it important to include in order to ensure a perfect world?**
- **Discuss the problems that might arise if we could create perfection.**

One of the difficulties you may have found when considering perfection is that we all have different ideas of what 'perfect' is. In Pleasantville USA, it's always 72 degrees fahrenheit and sunny. Every house has a white picket fence and a mum who has dinner on the table at 6pm sharp. The high school basketball team has never lost a game – in fact, it has never missed a basket. Nothing ever changes. This may or may not be your idea of perfection. Do you find the thought of nothing ever changing frightening or attractive?

Reese Witherspoon (Jennifer) underlined the symbolic importance of the blank books, for example, in Pleasantville's library.

'I think the blank books are a metaphor for the entire film. It's like all these people with covers that are beautiful and well adorned, but there's nothing really on the inside ... when they start reading and learning more about themselves ... their insides fill in and start to turn to colour ... It's really about finding individuality and identity.'

As with the other texts that we have studied, *Pleasantville* operates on several different levels. Metaphor and allegory are important in terms of communicating a number of complex ideas. It can be enjoyed as a simple adventure fantasy but it also rewards a deeper analysis of the way in which it works.

3 **Watch the sequence in the early part of the film that shows David and Jennifer arriving in Pleasantville. At first the town of Pleasantville seems perfect.**
- **What kinds of images are used?**
- **What kind of values do they represent?**

The town in the television sitcom is an 'ideal' American community – it presents one idea of how some Americans liked to see the world in the 1950s. It also raises important questions about how people live in communities – how do we tolerate people who are different to us? Is some conflict good for the health of the community? Similar questions are raised in both *The Crucible* (US, 1996) and *To Kill a Mockingbird* (US, 1962).

Gary Ross made his film partly to help restore the reputation of his father – one of the scriptwriters who suffered from persecution during the McCarthy witch-hunts in Hollywood in the late 1940s and early 1950s.

4 **Think carefully about what happens in the film.**
- **How does conformity work in *Pleasantville*?**
- **How are David and Jennifer made to feel?**

5 **Ideas can be represented allegorically in many ways.**
- **What does Jennifer think about the clothes she is expected to wear as Mary Sue?**
- **Can you explain how the norms of behaviour in Pleasantville could be seen as a form of persecution?**

Colour is an important metaphor in *Pleasantville* – it carries a number of complex meanings. It also sets up puzzles for the audience to work out. Why are people changing colour? As with another film, *The Wizard of Oz* (US, 1939), colour is used to define two different worlds and to express emotional shifts inside the film's characters.

6 **Many scenes in *Pleasantville* rely on the clever use of colour. Watch the sequence in which Betty Parker covers up her 'shameful' new colours with black-and-white makeup – only to have her tears wash parts of it away revealing the colour to Mr Johnson (approx. 66 minutes into the film).**
- **Look at the use of close-ups on her face. What effect do these have upon the audience?**

PLEASANTVILLE

7 The soundtrack and the acting also emphasise the emotions in the scene.
- What changes do you see in Betty as her new face is revealed?

8 Think about the changes in Betty's character as the film develops. She begins as a fictional creation of the perfect, unquestioning housewife, but she develops from a two-dimensional character to three dimensions.
- What causes these changes?
- How are they shown?
- What kinds of social comments are being made about the position of women in the 1950s and today, through her character?

Reese Witherspoon who plays Jennifer said that 'Jennifer goes through a lot of different phases in the film. In Pleasantville, she realises that she doesn't have to base her identity on her sexuality and constantly trying to conform.'

The differences between individuals and their needs are explored through the character of Jennifer. For Betty the colour of the 'real world' means liberation – for Jennifer the black-and-white world allows her to define herself through her intellect rather than her appearance/sexuality.

9 Can you give examples from the film of how the director shows us these changes in Betty and Jennifer/Mary Sue's behaviour?

Gary Ross stated that what is revealed in the film is the opposites and extremes in life.
    'How can you know what beauty is if you don't know the opposite? How can you know what you really love if you're not in danger of losing it?'

10 Make a list of the opposites and extremes that you have noticed in the film.

11 Think about the characters of Jennifer and David.
- What are the oppositions evident in these characters?

PLEASANTVILLE

THE 1950s AND THE 1990s

With our understanding of history we can think about *Pleasantville* in terms of two views of America, represented by black-and-white television and colour Hollywood film. It seems fairly clear that Gary Ross sees the eruption of colour as a good thing, but is he really trying to tell us how the 1950s could be improved? As a general rule, films usually tell us something about now (ie the period when they were produced) even when they are set in the past.

12 Watch the closing sequence of the film.
- What might this sequence be telling us about the present?
- Are there other things that happen in the world of Pleasantville that could be seen as a criticism of contemporary America?
- What happens to David and Jennifer?
- What might this be saying about the two worlds represented in the film? What does it tell us about the two central characters?

13 The scene between David and his mother at the end of the film is very revealing.
- What does she tell him?
- How has David/Bud's relationship with Betty helped him to talk to his own mother?

REVIEWING THE FILM

Most American film critics liked *Pleasantville* and it did very well at the American box office. But some critics thought the film was 'heavy-handed' or 'over-reaching' in its attempts to make political comments about race relations and extreme political movements through gentle comedy. Some suggested that it had 'too many ideas'. What do you think?

BACKGROUND INFORMATION
The American TV Sitcom

Television began in America in the late 1940s and became extremely popular. It was felt to be one of the major benefits of post-war American life and a symbol of a new affluence. The programmes shown on television picked up on this idea of a modern America, shiny and new.

'Situation comedies', built around the home life of the typical American family, were very important. The family was 'wholesome' with father and mother, one son and one daughter. Mother stayed at home and looked after the family while father worked a nine-to-five job to earn the family income. Nothing 'bad' ever happened and the catchphrase 'Honey, I'm home!' summed up the predictability of the plot. William H Macey, who played the role of George in *Pleasantville*, said that one of the most interesting scenes for him to play was the first night when he comes home and Betty isn't there with the dinner waiting. When she doesn't reply to his 'Honey, I'm home' George tries again.

'He's trying to give Betty the cues for her behaviour – he's acting in his own life. And that's what we often do – things will be fine as long as we pick up each other's cues and know our lines. It's a great metaphor for America.'

14 To what extent are modern US sitcoms different to 'Pleasantville'?
■ Make a note of any family-based US sitcoms you have seen recently. Do they still represent the same typical US family?

15 Have British TV sitcoms followed the American pattern? One British sitcom with father, mother, son and daughter was called 'Two Point Four Children', seemingly commenting on the attempt to present a 'normal' family.
■ Make a list of British sitcoms centred on families. What do they say, if anything, about the modern British family?

LITERATURE, FILM AND CONSERVATIVE MORAL VALUES

In America, there are many small communities that have tried to protect their citizens from dangerous ideas – especially those coming from art and literature. The book that Mary Sue is reading in Pleasantville when she turns down a date is *Lady Chatterley's Lover* by D H Lawrence. This book was banned in both Britain and America because of the detailed description of the sexual relationship enjoyed by Lady Chatterley and her gamekeeper.

The scene in the film where the black-and-white people of Pleasantville burn all the books is an obvious reference to the book-burning carried out by the Nazis in Germany in the 1930s, when Hitler tried to stop people reading about communism and other beliefs he didn't share. In American small towns in the 1930s there were similar reactions to anything that challenged the accepted moral codes. On one famous occasion, a teacher was put on trial in the South for teaching about the evolution of the species. Books can be seen as dangerous because they communicate ideas that challenge the status quo.

16 To what extent is there still a threat that books or films may be banned today?
■ Are there strong moral constraints that mean that films that cross these boundaries (in terms of sex or violence, for example) are repressed?
■ Do writers, television producers and filmmakers still need to represent such beliefs allegorically in order to expose or challenge them?
■ You could find out what sorts of pressures filmmakers in Iran, for example, face in showing the problems of women in that society.
■ Or you could research whether filmmakers in Hollywood are influenced by pressures from large American religious groups. (One group sells specially edited video copies of popular films from which it has removed scenes which involve 'too much' sex or violence.)

Case Studies

THE CRUCIBLE

+ Student Notes & Activities +

You have already begun to explore *The Crucible* as an allegorical play. By setting the play in 1692 in Salem, Massachusetts and focusing upon the Salem witchcraft trials, Arthur Miller was able to make comments about what was happening in America during the period he was writing (the early 1950s). Anyone who opposed the authority of the Salem judges was automatically suspected of trying to undermine the court, in the same way Senator Joseph McCarthy accused anyone who opposed him of being a communist. The general atmosphere of suspicion aroused by McCarthy mirrored the panic and fear caused by the accusations of the hysterical Salem girls.

When *The Crucible* (US, 1996) was first produced many people saw it as a powerful comment on the problems of the time – Arthur Miller was using allegory to criticise policies, systems and political figures. These comments were important at the time and they help audiences to explore the importance of the historical background of any piece of art. However, now that these hearings are in the past we should also think about the qualities that make it important and relevant in the twenty-first century. We may want to interpret the allegory in a different way in the light of our changing knowledge, experience and understanding of the world.

THE CRUCIBLE

1 Can you think of any historical, religious, or political figures who have been oppressed because of their beliefs? Find out about one of these people and present your findings to the rest of the class. When you have identified several such figures, try to work out if they share any common characteristics.

2 Witches are not important in today's society. Can you think of any other groups of people who are met with responses such as fear, panic, suspicion or even hatred by other groups in society?

Arthur Miller adapted *The Crucible* for the cinema in 1996. He was excited, some forty years after writing the play on which the film is based, by the possibility of reaching a new, much wider audience. He was also anxious for us to think carefully about the parallels and connections that could be made in today's society. *The Crucible* can be enjoyed as an historical drama, just as the film *Pleasantville* (US, 1998) can be 'read' as a youth picture and a time travel fantasy. Both films, however, make it quite hard for us to be satisfied with a simple reading. They set problems up which we, the audience, are invited to solve or understand.

For example, in *Pleasantville* it is almost impossible to accept that some of the town's inhabitants are really black-and-white while others are coloured especially when some undergo the process of change before our eyes. Instead we see the use of colour as a code which we need to understand, in order to appreciate what the filmmaker is saying to us. Because human beings are problem solvers, we are used to decoding texts and interpreting signs on a day-to-day basis. In film we are constantly 'reading' the codes and conventions. For example we tend to associate the use of black-and-white with the past, or with documentaries. We accept that colour can be used as a symbol – red for passion, or danger, or hell.

CHARACTER

The central character in *The Crucible*, John Proctor, helps to raise issues of personal conscience and collective tyranny as he struggles to uphold his values in a society that seems determined to destroy him. He highlights common themes with which we can identify no matter what culture we live in. It is almost impossible not to search for parallels in modern society – you may not have heard of Senator Joe McCarthy but there are many other connections that you can make. For example, there are still many countries around the world where people are oppressed because of their religious or political beliefs.

A note on hysteria

Hysteria is a term that can be used in a number of different ways. In one sense it is a medical term with a very specific use in psychiatry. In more general usage it often refers to extremely emotional and irrational behaviour. 'Mass hysteria' is where a whole community acts emotionally and without thinking clearly. The word can also be used in a derogatory way, and has often been used dismiss women who make demands on others or society in general. The word is derived from the Greek word for 'womb' and some people used to believe that the psychological condition was biological in origin and confined to women.

The power of hysteria is central to the play. Is the kind of mass hysteria we witness in the text evident in contemporary society?

3 Some people have argued that the public displays of grief when Princess Diana was killed in 1997 were a form of mass hysteria (but others thought this was quite healthy). You could consider the wave of euphoria that swept the country during the 2002 Football World Cup.
- Did you display the England flag from your window?
- Were your lessons cancelled to allow you to watch certain matches?
- What was the atmosphere like if you watched in a large group situation?
- How did you feel if you weren't interested in football and didn't care whether England won or lost?
- To what extent do you think people's behaviour during the World Cup was hysterical?

THE CRUCIBLE

In *The Crucible* the young girls who danced in the woods worked themselves up into a state of hysteria, which ended up infecting the whole community. They lived in a very repressive society, a narrow world where they had little outlet for their energies and frustrations. Our society is very different to theirs but being a teenager isn't easy and so it is understandable that young people might want to rebel by doing things that figures of authority (parents, teachers) would not approve of. We also know how important peer group pressure is. Often we will do things in a group that we would not think of doing on our own. So it is possible to identify at some level with the central character of Abigail, while at the same time recognising that she is acting irrationally.

SETTING

After the opening of his play, Arthur Miller re-designed the set to consist of simple black drapes and strong, white, static lighting. The setting of any production can affect the way in which the audience responds to the text. The dark, claustrophobic world of *The Crucible* expresses the stifling emotional world, suspicion, dark thoughts and deeds and the rising hysteria as events unfold.

Most productions of the play concentrate on indoor settings, but the film version, directed by Nicholas Hytner, uses the woods and scenery of New England so we are given a much wider picture of the setting.

4 Why do you think the setting has been extended in the film?

In a film visual imagery and sound are important ways of 'carrying over meaning'. In a play it is usually the spoken word that carries the metaphorical and allegorical elements. During the opening of Act One, Reverend Samuel Parris describes Tituba in the woods,

THE CRUCIBLE

'And I heard her screeching and gibberish coming from her mouth. She was swaying like a dumb beast over that fire!' We do not see the rituals in the wood, they are described to us by Parris. We 'see' the incident through his eyes.

5a Read through the opening of The Crucible, stopping when John Proctor enters. We are told in the stage directions that a sense of confusion surrounds Parris and he seems about to weep. The dialogue creates the feeling of a growing hysteria. Now watch the opening sequence of the film again (approx. four minutes).
■ What are the major differences? What are the similarities?

5b The play reveals the pagan ritual in the woods through Reverend Parris' dialogue – the full story of the events of that night remains shrouded in secrecy throughout the play. The film includes this scene in its opening sequence.
■ How does this affect our view of what is to follow?
■ Why do you think the director, Nicholas Hytner, chose to include the scene?
■ How is the film's language used to create a feeling of hysteria? Does the film do anything that the play does not?

Lily Kilvert, the production designer for the film, said that she wanted to create

> 'a feeling that here was a world that was incredibly perfect and so tragic to lose.'

Considerable time and care was taken to reproduce the village of Salem. The setting was carefully researched. Architecture, costumes and even the plants and animals were historically correct. In contrast to the stark stage set, the visual look of the film is beautiful. The contrast between the opening sequences of the play and the film helps to emphasise how different ways of using visual metaphor can create and 'carry over' meaning.

6 Watch the opening sequence of the film. What elements of it suggest the supernatural?

7 If you had no previous knowledge of the text, which genre of film would you think it was?

8a Now watch the closing sequence of the film once more from the point where John Proctor's confession is obtained (approximately one hour, 43 minutes). The scene is set against a New England skyline with a 'backdrop' of leafless, gnarled trees. John Proctor is shown travelling in a wooden cart with his two fellow prisoners. He has refused to allow his confession to be nailed onto the church door.

- Look carefully at how the prisoners are represented (costume, clothes, make up etc).
- Think about the symbolism of the cart and the gallows.
- How does the environment reflect the inner emotions of the characters?

8b The film ends with the three prisoners reciting The Lord's Prayer.

- What do you notice about the sound levels whilst they are praying? Why does John Proctor emphasise certain lines?
- How is the camera used to highlight the emotions of the crowd surrounding the gallows? What effect do these close-ups have upon us, the audience?

9 John Proctor is the central character in the film. It is through his character that we are encouraged to consider the relationship between the individual and society.

- Choose three contrasting sequences that show aspects of Proctor's personality, for example, his exchanges with his wife at the beginning of the film, his encounter with Abigail in the woods, his final moments with his wife towards the close of the film.
- How is the film's language used to help create an understanding of the importance of his name to his sense of self-identity?

THE CRUCIBLE

ACTORS AND STARS

The film of *The Crucible* is able to reach a much wider audience than any single stage production. Part of the appeal of the film is the appearance of 'star actors'. The three leading figures in the film are all worth considering in terms of how their 'star image' supports (or contradicts) the meaning of the text, and thereby reinforces the power of the allegory.

10 Find out some of the other roles played by Daniel Day Lewis, Joan Allen and Winona Ryder. The Internet Movie Database at http://uk.imdb.com and fan websites should provide you with a lot of information.

- Do you think that the roles were well cast?
- What do these stars bring to their roles?

TO KILL A MOCKINGBIRD

Case Studies

TO KILL A MOCKINGBIRD

─────────────── + Student Notes & Activities + ───────────────

The use of allegory and metaphor in Harper Lee's novel and the subsequent film directed by Robert Mulligan (1962) is slightly more deeply buried than in *The Crucible*. However, there are similarities between the texts. Both Harper Lee and Arthur Miller were writing in America in the 1950s. Both reflected in some way the effect of the Great Depression on American society. Oppression and injustice are important themes. There is a tension between the way things appear and the way they really are.

The image of the mockingbird is an important 'key' to unlocking some of the important ideas, themes, and social, historical and cultural comments contained within *To Kill a Mockingbird*. An analysis could begin with the title.

TO KILL A MOCKINGBIRD

1 **What kind of bird is a mockingbird? Does it have any unusual characteristics?**

If you have already read the novel you may have discovered that the mockingbird has no original song of its own. Instead it mimics the song of other birds. The song of the mockingbird is therefore a useful metaphor for the opinions voiced by the people in the town of Maycomb, Alabama – they don't have a voice of their own, they just 'sing' the traditional beliefs of the community, which in this case are racist. So, if we take this 'reading', 'to kill a mockingbird' would be to stop the voice of the crowd, to stop the repetition of traditional views and to allow the voice of individual 'birds' to be heard.

However, it is important to remember that different readers can interpret a metaphor in different ways. For example, we may instead want to compare the characters of both Tom Robinson and Boo Radley with this bird. They are both gentle people who have done no harm but only try to help others. Both are persecuted, one by the jury and the other by gossips. Like the mockingbird they should be protected and cared for. Instead, they are hunted down by a mob intoxicated by false courage and ignorance – like the children who shoot songbirds. Whatever our reading, it is clear that the mockingbird links important themes in the book: justice and childhood.

The family at the centre of the story are the Finches. The different readings of the words of the title are hinted at during the title sequence and opening scenes of the film.

2 **Watch the title sequence only. Concentrate hard on what you are shown and make a list of what is shown.**
- **Why do you think the camera pans across the series of objects?**
- **From your understanding of the book are any of these objects important?**
- **What happens to the child's drawing of a bird? What could this symbolise?**

3 **Now watch the opening scene up to the point when Mr. Cunningham leaves on his horse and cart. What elements of the film's language are used to establish atmosphere and setting? Who 'tells' the story at first?**

Harper Lee, who was born in Monroeville, Alabama in 1926, wrote *To Kill a Mockingbird*. She studied Law at the University of Alabama and wrote this, her first novel, in New York. It was published in 1960, at the time when the Civil Rights movement was being encouraged by the presidential election campaign of John F Kennedy. The story is set in the 1930s during the time of the Great Depression when there was great hardship and when the 'Jim Crow' laws in Alabama were unchallenged. (At the end of this case study are notes about the struggle for Civil Rights and the 'Jim Crow' laws).

4 **The metaphor involving the mockingbird helps draws the story together and to give it deeper meanings. Watch the scene where young Walter is invited to dinner with the Finches after his fight with Scout on her first day at school (approx. 36 minutes from beginning of tape).**
- **Why does Atticus talk about the mockingbird?**
- **What are the important characteristics of the bird?**
- **How is the importance of understanding others expressed during the conversation between Scout and Atticus on the back porch?**
- **What is revealed about Calpurnia's role in the family and how does this 'fit in' with issues raised in the film?**

TO KILL A MOCKINGBIRD

THE 'REAL' STORY

The central action of the story, as with *The Crucible*, refers to a real incident, one of the most famous trials in American legal history, held in Scottsville, Alabama between 1931 and 1937. Nine black teenagers were charged with raping two white women who had been with them (and some white men) travelling in a freight car on the railroad. The trial exposed to many Americans the unfair treatment of black men in Southern courts. The black teenagers' lawyer questioned the women about their behaviour and was severely reprimanded by the judge for doubting the reputation of white Southern women. At that time sexual relationships between people of different races were seen as unacceptable because they appeared to threaten the social stability of white society in the South.

In *To Kill a Mockingbird* the people of Maycomb also are so deeply entrenched in their prejudice that they do not realise their own hypocrisy. The double standards so clearly underlined during Aunt Alexandra's missionary circle tea reflect the double standards of America both in the 1930s and the 1950s. The women talk with great sympathy about the plight of poor tribes in Africa but later condemn the dissatisfaction of the Negroes in their own town. At school, Miss Gates extols the virtue of American democracy, then complains that the Negroes are 'getting way above themselves'.

Clearly then, Harper Lee was saying something important about American society. However, when looking at all of the films in these Case Studies, it has been stressed that any work of art must say something about the contemporary world known to the audience at the time when the film was made. This means that we should try to think about whether the same double standards about the treatment of black people in America were evident in the 1960s as well as the 1930s.

5 Can you think of any examples of double standards, either in our society or in terms of the freedom and democracy so widely heralded in America?

VIEWPOINTS

The hero of the novel is Scout – she also narrates the story. The novel gives us two different viewpoints, the older Scout retelling incidents from her childhood and the younger Scout, who is six at the beginning and nine when the story ends. The language of the book is adult in style and yet often she relates incidents that she does not fully understand. This device encourages the reader to work hard. It adds depth to the narrative, as we have to think about what Scout can't explain. It also allows us to look at the story through a child's eyes as she becomes aware of injustice and prejudice for the first time.

6 When you watch the film try to decide whose 'eyes' we are seeing the story through.
- Does the view change during certain parts of the film?
- Is Scout still the hero of the story or does this change also?

7 If you decide that Scout is no longer the 'hero' consider the reasons for the change. Gregory Peck was a very popular Hollywood star in 1962 when the film was made.
- Do you think this may have influenced any change in emphasis in terms of the central character?

8 It has been suggested that To Kill a Mockingbird was Harper Lee's way of exploring the events of the late 1950s, such as the Little Rock High School incident (see notes at the end), in order that readers could think through the issues more clearly when presented through the eyes of a child.
- How are the issues presented clearly through the film's language? Pick one or two incidents from the film and describe the ways in which the film language emphasises the issues being dealt with.

The theme of the novel is the growing maturity of the Finch children who learn to confront their fears and to deal with the world. Yet it was set in the 1930s and although Atticus is a liberal and defends a black man accused of rape, he is still unable to comprehend that the system of segregation must be opposed and brought to an end – the mockingbird must be silenced. Scout does in a child's way recognise injustice and she is outspoken, so she creates the possibility of change. By writing about the 1930s during the 1960s, Harper Lee was enabling many Americans to think about the racism and injustice that was still evident in their country.

TO KILL A MOCKINGBIRD

9 Look at the final sequence from the film. Begin when the sheriff tells Atticus that Bob Ewell's death must have been an accident.
- How are the ideas about the mockingbird revisited?
- How does Scout use the metaphor to persuade Atticus to cover up the facts surrounding Ewell's death?
- How has Scout 'grown' during the two years?
- How far has she been able to 'stand in others' shoes'?

NOTES ON THE HISTORICAL CONTEXT
The Great Depression

During the 1930s there was a major economic crisis throughout the world. People in rural America were particularly badly affected, with farmers going bankrupt, banks failing and millions out of work. This situation lasted for most of the decade and many Americans were deeply scarred by their experiences.

Jim Crow

The term 'Jim Crow' refers to the whole system of laws and administration created by state governments in the American South in the 1880s. The name comes from a minstrel character (white performers 'blacking up' as 'nigger minstrels' was a popular form of entertainment from the 1820s onwards). The laws created segregation and meant that for black people the 'liberation' from slavery supposedly brought about by the Civil War, which ended in 1865, were rendered meaningless. These laws were not challenged by the federal government in Washington until the 1950s.

The struggle for civil rights

The Jim Crow laws meant that black people were not allowed to use the same facilities as whites. In South Africa a similar system of laws produced apartheid or 'separation'; the preferred American term was 'segregation'. During the 1950s, black people began to fight for their right to be treated equally before the law. Their claims to equal treatment were supported by the decisions of the federal court in Washington and opposed by the white governors of states like Mississippi, Louisiana and Arkansas.

The struggles were about the rights of black people to:
- Ride on the same buses and use the same seats as white people;
- Go to the same schools and colleges and use the same libraries as white people;
- Eat at the same lunch stands and use the same hotels as white people (black musicians were prevented from touring with whites).

In addition, at the national level, the entertainment industry treated black and white audiences as completely separate and films and records were distributed to one or the other, but not both.

Organisations like the NAACP (The National Association for the Advancement of Colored People) were important in fighting legal battles. Demonstrations and marches were organised mainly by church leaders like the Reverend Martin Luther King. Many individuals became heroes of the struggle like Rosa Parks who, in 1955, started the 'Bus Boycott' in Montgomery, Alabama, when she refused to give up her seat to a white passenger.

TO KILL A MOCKINGBIRD

Little Rock High School

In 1957, nine black teenagers attempted to enrol at a 'white' High School in Little Rock, Arkansas. State National Guards were posted to prevent them entering. The federal government in Washington sent troops to force the Governor of Arkansas to allow them in.

The Civil Rights struggles of the 1950s eventually led black voters to help the Democratic candidate John F Kennedy win the 1960 presidential election. He promised a Civil Rights Bill to change laws throughout America and although Kennedy was assassinated in 1963, the laws were passed by his successor, Lyndon Baines Johnson.

The language of racism

The term 'Negro' was used by both white and black people in America up to the time of the Civil Rights movement and so we have used it in relation to the language of the book and the film. In the 1960s, Black people in America began to call themselves 'black', arguing that 'negro' was a term from the days of slavery. Later the accepted term became African-American and now some people use the term 'people of colour'.

KES

Case Studies

KES

— ┼ Student Notes & Activities ┼ —

In this Case Study you are invited to consider how Billy Casper's experience of training his kestrel is a metaphor for how Billy himself is 'trained' or 'socialised' into living in his own community.

The film *Kes* (UK, 1969) was adapted for the screen by Barry Hines from his book *A Kestrel for a Knave* written in 1968. Kes is the name of the kestrel that young Billy Casper trains – the relationship between the bird and Billy is central to both texts. *Kes* focuses on British society during the late 1960s, but covers similar issues to the other films looked at in this course.

KES

On a personal level, we are told the story of Billy Casper, a young lad who catches and trains a hawk. It is through Billy, however, that Barry Hines makes social comments about the education system, the family and the wasted potential of so many people living in northern, working class communities during that period in history. The title of the novel points directly to an allegorical meaning. In feudal England there was a strict hierarchy. The ruling class, the nobles, were allowed to keep the most noble hunting bird, the peregrine falcon. The knave, a person of much lower rank, was allowed to keep a 'lesser' hawk, the kestrel.

The film is not an allegory, at least not in the way the other films we are discussing are allegorical. Ken Loach, the film's director, tried to make the film as realistic as possible, using a real setting (a school in Barnsley, for example) and real people (David Bradley who played Billy was a pupil at the school). Some of the scenes use ordinary people, rather than actors, and improvised dialogue. The film sets out first of all to tell the story of a boy who trains a kestrel. Loach wants us to believe in the truth of the

KES

story and then to make up our own minds what wider meaning it has in terms of highlighting issues in British society. For Loach, the story itself carries the meaning – it isn't necessary to 'decode' the symbols. Nevertheless, the metaphors are there to allow us to make connections and to help us to have a closer understanding of Billy's emotional world as well as his social world. Films do not always mean what the filmmaker intends – sometimes audiences make them mean something else. Films do not always work for an audience in the way that the filmmakers intend. Watching *Kes*, some audiences will think more about Billy's emotional world and other audiences will think about the social conditions in which Billy must live.

1 **For your initial research, try to find out about kestrels.**

2 **Billy tells Mr Farthing at one point that the reason Kes is so 'great' is because he can't be tamed. 'It's fierce an' wild, an' it's not bothered about anybody, not even about me, right.'**
- **Think about Billy and the way he lives: what connections might you make between the lives of Billy and Kes?**
- **Does the bird help to reveal important things about Billy's past, present or future?**

Kes is more than a bird that Billy trains, it is a symbol of potential strength and freedom. Billy can 'train' the bird but he cannot own him – he does not want a pet – he wants something that is wild and free, something 'untameable'. From the earliest moments in the book and the film Billy is adamant that he won't become a miner and go down the pit. But that is what he is being 'trained' for. The bird is a metaphor for the 'training' of Billy by the community in which he lives. In the film, the pit looms in the background of numerous shots as a constant reminder of Billy's future. The contrast between the pit and the natural surroundings is emphasised by the cinematography[1].

---

1 Cinematography refers not only to what is filmed but how it is filmed: how the event is photographed and framed and how long the image lasts on the screen.

REPRESENTATION, REALISM & FANTASY: Case Studies

KES

Billy is frequently shown in the centre of the frame using a medium long shot. So he seems even smaller than he is and his isolation is underlined. Kes is rarely seen in close-up but is invariably shown as part of the natural world. The bird is a constant reminder of the potential that Billy has – with the right kind of nurturing he too could 'fly'.

3 Read through the short section of the novel that deals with Mr Gryce's assembly and finishes with the caning of the smokers. Watch the corresponding section of the film (approximately 57 minutes into the film).

- Concentrate on the similarities and differences between the texts. The 'smoker's scene' is much sadder and funnier in the film. In the book the little boy who has been sent to give a message to Mr Gryce is not described, he is simply called 'boy'.
- Think about the ways in which representation in this scene in the film help to add a different 'level'.
- How is the film's language used to evoke sympathy for the little boy?
- How does the caning of the innocent lad help to underline important comments made by Hines about the education system?

4 You will notice that in the novel the assembly is interspersed with Billy's daydreams about his hawk.
- How does the film sequence differ from the novel?
- Why do you think the assembly and subsequent events are shown as a continuous, chronological narrative in the film?

5 Why do you think Barry Hines chose to use the 'flashback, day-dreaming' device in the novel? One of Billy's daydreams begins as the children begin to recite The Lord's Prayer. Religious imagery is an important way of creating meaning in the book. There are several references to God the father, church, silence and reverence. When you read the book take note of the number of references to 'father'. God is the father, Jud and Billy don't have the same father, and the librarian needs to have Billy's father's signature before she will allow Billy to borrow a book.

KES

It isn't until the end of the novel that we realise the importance of references to religion and fatherhood. Billy's 'stream of consciousness' memories help us to piece together parts of Billy's past. Billy's memories appear as clips from a film. Billy as hero. Billy on screen. Big Billy. Kes on his own. Big Kes. Close-up. Technicolour. Ironically, when adapting his novel for the screen Barry Hines leaves out the scene at 'The Palace' and the cinematic references.

7 In small groups, read through the final five paragraphs of A Kestrel for a Knave.
- Why do you think Billy 'replays' these fragments of his past in the abandoned cinema?
- What is the story that emerges?
- What parts does Billy see himself and Kes playing in his 'Big Picture'?

8 Now review the final scene from Kes. The parts in the 'Big Picture' seem to have changed.
- How are Billy and Kes represented?
The endings seem to differ markedly.
- Can you think of reasons why Billy's past may be less important in terms of the film's narrative?

9 Read through the final paragraph of the book.
'It had stopped raining. The clouds were breaking up and stars showed in the spaces between them. Billy stood for a while glancing up and down the City Road, then he started to walk back the way he had come. When he arrived home there was no one in. He buried the hawk in the field just behind the shed; went in and went to bed.'
- Compare these final sentences and the close of the film. They seem very similar and yet it could be argued that the novel ends more hopefully than the film. Do you agree?

10 The book and the film were created in the 1960s and set during the same period of time.
- Do they have anything to tell us about our world today?
- To what extent are schools different today? How important is family, class, wealth and education in terms of young people's life chances? How important is the need to have something to care for or something in life that you can do well?

6 Watch the scene when Mr. Farthing goes to visit Billy in order to see him flying his hawk. Consider the use of film language – sound, camera work, editing and *mise en scéne*[2]. How is the feeling of reverence for the bird conveyed?

Barry Hines does not change the dialogue in this scene: both Billy and Mr Farthing talk about the feelings of respect and awe that Kes evokes, using religious terms. Mr Farthing says

'… it's as though it's flying in a pocket of silence … and this feeling, this silence, it must carry over. Have you noticed how quietly we're speaking? And how strange it sounded when I first raised my voice? It was almost like shouting in church.'

---

2 *Mise en scene* refers to literally everything that is put into the scene to be photographed. This usually includes set, location, actors, costume, make up, gesture, and use of colour and props.

Case Studies

THE WIZARD OF OZ

—— + Student Notes & Activities + ——

You have probably seen part or all of this film on television as it is shown regularly at Christmas and other holiday times. It was made in 1939 when colour films were still a novelty, but it has remained popular and has become known as a classic. We've included it here for a number of reasons:

- It could be seen as a forerunner of the modern 'youth picture'. We would say that Dorothy is a teenager, but in the 1930s the term hadn't yet been invented.
- In its use of colour and black-and-white, the film is an inspiration for *Pleasantville*.
- The way in which metaphor and allegory are used is very similar to classical literary works such as *The Pilgrim's Progress*.
- Several images and lines of dialogue from the film have been used many times over in the last 60 years, eg 'follow the Yellow Brick Road' and 'Toto, I've a feeling we're not in Kansas any more'.

THE WIZARD OF OZ

NOTE ON JUDY GARLAND

Judy Garland started as a child star, and remained a star all her life. *The Wizard of Oz* established her major stardom. In many ways she was the forerunner of modern stars such as Britney Spears and Kylie Minogue but, unlike them, she had little chance of controlling her life or her 'image'. The film studio, MGM, ruled her life and ruined her health with prescription drugs to control her weight. She married many times and died unhappy, aged only 47. Compared to the other films we are using as case studies, *The Wizard of Oz* seems to be much more concerned with universal values and ideas rather than a specific time period like the 1930s or 1950s. The story was written by L Frank Baum at the end of the nineteenth century and adapted as a play in 1901. The 1939 film was just one (the most celebrated) of many films and television programmes made from the same set of stories since the 1910s. However, we have stressed in various parts of this pack that films are always

THE WIZARD OF OZ

NOTE ON *THE PILGRIM'S PROGRESS*

Written by John Bunyan and published between 1678 and 1684, *The Pilgrim's Progress* is a religious allegory in the form of a dream by the author. The hero, Christian, finds himself fleeing from the City of Destruction and looking for the Celestial City. On his journey he meets several characters such as Mr Wordly-Wise, Faithful, Hopeful and Giant Despair.

about 'now', whenever they are made. So, a film made in 1939 must in some way be influenced by the Great Depression of the 1930s and the sense of a world war looming not far ahead.

THE WIZARD OF OZ

Setting

The film begins in the mid-West, the centre of the United States. When Dorothy arrives in the fantasy land of Oz, her reference back to Kansas is a recognition that she has moved away from the 'ordinary' and 'known' world.

Dorothy

She represents the 'ordinary' people of America. She is a 'simple' country girl, not stupid, but not very 'worldly-wise'. (Superman is another American hero who grows up on a little farm in the mid-West.)

The Wicked Witch of the East

She represents the bankers and industrialists of the big Eastern cities like New York, who many people believed, exploited rural workers (and who in the 1930s were the real villains for farmers who lost their land).

The Cowardly Lion

This character refers directly to a politician, but could equally be anybody who makes brave speeches, but who inside is frightened and doesn't really believe they can do anything.

The Tin Man

The industrial worker is represented by this 'mechanical man' who is treated by the industrialists as if he were a machine. When Dorothy finds him he is unable to move, having 'rusted up' when he was left out in the rain.

The Wizard

Pretending to be a 'Great Wizard', but in reality just an ordinary man, this character was based on another politician who Baum thought was just a front for someone who was 'pulling the strings'. Many American presidents have been characters like this. To get elected they need millions of dollars and their unknown sponsors, who control this money, have the power to influence governments, behind the scenes.

For many years, *The Wizard of Oz* was accepted mainly as a children's story. Many adults recognised that it was an allegory, but it wasn't obvious exactly what Baum had been trying to say and what the many symbols might refer to. In 1964 a teacher, Henry Littlefield, and his high school students produced a detailed explanation of the allegory as they saw it. Frank Baum, they claimed, wrote the story to criticise the political scene in America in the 1890s. Since 1964, the story has been widely studied as an allegory.

It would take too long here to explain American politics in the 1890s and some of the issues are bewildering to a UK readership (eg the 'yellow brick road' refers to the place of gold in the currency system). But many of the other symbols are much easier to understand and they do have a more 'universal' application. Here are some of the suggestions:

1 Watch the sequence when Dorothy first arrives in Oz and meets the Scarecrow.
- What kind of character is the scarecrow?
- How is he presented in visual terms and by the music sequence?
- What kinds of 'universal values' do we associate with this kind of character?

The political philosophy that Baum investigated in his stories was Populism and in the 1890s it had many followers in the mid-West. As the name suggests, it was a movement of 'ordinary people' – farmers, small business people and trades people. Dorothy represents these people who have basic 'common sense' but neither the knowledge of politics or the confidence in their own strengths and abilities which could allow them to triumph over the 'fat cats' of big business. Baum thought they should find that confidence and that is what the film is about. Together, Dorothy, the Tin Man, the Scarecrow and the Cowardly Lion help each other to overcome their weaknesses.

The Wizard of Oz is one of the most important and most loved examples of children's literature in the United States. In 1978 an African-American version of the film, *The Wiz*, was released with Diana Ross as Dorothy and Michael Jackson as the Scarecrow. Earlier in 1973, Elton John produced a best-selling album called

THE WIZARD OF OZ

'Goodbye Yellow Brick Road'. The title track refers to a young man who has 'left the farm' in search of fame and fortune, but who now thinks he should head back home.

2 Think about the power of the idea of the 'yellow brick road' in an American context.

- Why is it important that Dorothy is a girl from a farm in the mid-West?
- Why is the image of the road leading into the distance so powerful for young Americans?

GENRE

The main genre references in *The Wizard of Oz* are the musical and the road movie. These are both genres very much associated with American culture. One critic has argued that the musical is very much concerned with ideas of 'abundance' and celebration – it is certainly a genre in which there are great displays of energy and also of spectacle. It could be argued that Americans show confidence in their country through the vitality of the musical. The road movie is slightly more ambiguous in its allegorical possibilities. It is commonly regarded as *the* American genre partly because America is a very big country with wide-open spaces. America invented the car culture and Americans tend to travel within their own country more than most other nationalities. The road movie is ambiguous because the characters who set out on a journey are either escaping from one situation or desperately searching for something else.
The motivation to travel may be different in each case, but the effect is the same. Making a journey means meeting new people and new situations. Inevitably, characters learn about themselves in the process, discovering themselves as they discover new places. It is something of a cliché, but the road is a metaphor for life.

3 Is Dorothy 'leaving to forget' or 'hoping to discover something new'?

- What do you think she discovers about herself?

4 List any other films that you think use elements from the 'road movie'.

- What are the characters trying to escape or find out about in each case?

REPRESENTATION, REALISM & FANTASY: Case Studies

Case Studies

BUFFY THE VAMPIRE SLAYER

+ Student Notes & Activities +

Buffy the Vampire Slayer (BTVS) became a successful television series, almost 'coming back from the dead' after the original feature film flopped at the cinema in 1992. In its television guise, the story of Buffy and her friends succeeded partly because a television series allows characters to develop (and audiences to get to know them) over a relatively long period. Changing storylines over several years, which give the characters new challenges to face, help maintain the viewers' interest in them.

A NOTE ABOUT TELEVISION SERIES

There are several different ways in which stories on television have traditionally been presented – as a:

- 'single story' (like a film);
- soap opera ('continuous' stories, shown several times a week);
- serial (one story spread over several episodes, with a clear beginning and end);
- series (separate stories each week over a number of weeks).

In America, a successful series will run for several years, with a season of anything up to twenty-six episodes each year. BTVS began in 1997 and is still running at the time of writing these notes.

BTVS, like much of modern television, borrows ideas from other types of programmes – in this case the serial and soap opera. Over a season there is usually a single big story running all the way through, with separate small stories in each episode. Allied to this are two distinctive features which mark out BTVS as different:

- The characters in the series grow older, as in real life. Buffy starts off in high school and then goes on to 'college' – she and her friends grow up;
- The series combines two genres – horror and youth picture, so Buffy fights demons and struggles with being a teenage girl and young woman at the same time.

BUFFY: ALLEGORY AND METAPHOR

In BTVS, the main characters are faced with vampires and other assorted 'demons' who are attacking the young people of Sunnydale, a town unfortunately built over the Hellmouth – the entrance to the 'Underworld'. The word 'demon' usually means an evil spirit (but it can also mean 'genius'). Throughout history, most societies have recognised that some people behave in ways that are dangerous to themselves and to others – they seem 'possessed' by something. This was explained as possession by demons. Many religions refer to evil spirits and the most famous European story concerns the character, Faust, who agreed to 'sell' his soul to the Devil in return for 'earthly pleasures'. The Faust story points to the idea of temptation – and the price we may pay to get what we want.

Literature has developed different kinds of stories related to these ideas. In some the demons are 'real', like the Devil, in others human characters suffer from 'inner demons' – urges, desires and temptations they must face up to and either give in to or resist. BTVS combines both kinds of stories. Vampires must be slain, but all the anxieties of being an adolescent must be faced as well.

1 It's worth stopping at this point to think about the 'demons' you face as a teenager. What do you find most difficult to deal with? Are you tempted to do things that you think you shouldn't? Probably you want to keep any temptations secret – or perhaps discuss them with a few very close friends. Most of us are like this. What do you notice about your friends and their demons? Try to jot down a few general points about what kinds of 'troubles' most teenagers face. The chances are that BTVS will feature at least one of these as the central feature of an episode.

BTVS works so well in linking the 'real' demons and the 'inner demons' because it is able to draw on the extensive use of metaphors in the horror genre. The modern horror film has its roots in the eighteenth and nineteenth centuries when women were not supposed to be seen to enjoy sexual experiences and certainly not to display any interest in sexual activity. Stories about blood-sucking vampires, like *Dracula* written by Bram Stoker in the 1890s, were read avidly by women who saw the vampire as an illicit romantic hero. The deadly embrace of the vampire with the bite into the neck was taken to be a metaphor for the sexual act of penetration of the woman – showing blood was acceptable in a society that wouldn't accept overt representations of sexuality.

A second metaphor also developed very early on. This was the idea that the vampire spread a plague. In the nineteenth century all kinds of infectious diseases were still rampant in Europe, but recently the metaphor has been taken to refer to sexually transmitted diseases (STDs) and in particular HIV/AIDS. STDs have also been given a moral dimension by social commentators who blame them on 'promiscuous behaviour', especially by young people.

It isn't difficult to see how these various factors combine in one of the strongest stories in BTVS – Buffy's relationship with Angel, the reformed vampire. We can see that by 'despatching' the demons of Sunnydale, Buffy is, within the metaphor, controlling her own sexual desire (resisting the vampire's 'kiss') and being socially responsible. When she falls for Angel, her vision becomes less 'black and white'. Real life is much messier than a simple tale of good and bad. A young woman trying to decide whether or not to sleep with her boyfriend has to weigh up a whole range of different 'rights and wrongs'. For many critics, what makes BTVS such a good series is that it both takes issues very seriously and manages to do so with a 'light touch'. Each episode shifts seemingly effortless from danger to comic relief. What can seem like a matter of life and death one minute can be almost forgotten very soon afterwards. These mood changes are also, in a way, an allegory for teenage life.

The two episodes from BTVS discussed below have been chosen because they offer good examples of the use of metaphors which link the demon threat and the inner demons of teenage life. You should be able to find similar metaphors at work in many other episodes.

BUFFY THE VAMPIRE SLAYER

A METAPHOR FOR STRUGGLES OVER 'IDENTITY' – WHO IS THE 'REAL ME'?

Series 2 Episode 15: 'Phases'

This episode combines a classic horror story – the tale of the werewolf – with the issue of young males and their insecurity about their own sexuality. Willow has fallen for Oz, but he doesn't seem that interested. However, he is teased and bullied by a gang led by Larry because of his relationship with Willow. Buffy and Xander try to help Willow. Buffy can do 'girl talk', but Xander tries to be macho and he confronts Larry. Because he thinks that Xander has discovered his secret, Larry blurts out that he is gay, thus one identity has been resolved. Meanwhile,

Sunnydale has been terrorised by a werewolf during the full moon. Larry had been the number one suspect, but it turns out to be Oz who is transformed each night. Buffy is just in time to prevent a bounty hunter killing Oz and Willow finally tranquillises him when he is about to attack her. Despite the attack, Willow says she will accept Oz 'as he is'.

REPRESENTATION, REALISM & FANTASY: Case Studies

This episode explores a central problem of school life for all students – 'peer group pressure'. We often tend to worry about what everyone else will think if they discover that we are 'different' in some way. But hiding that difference can be more dangerous than confronting it. Larry 'comes out' as gay and Oz is discovered to be a werewolf. Both find a measure of acceptance that is better than the fear of being 'found out'.

2 In groups, discuss the importance of 'peer group' pressure in school.
- What are the most important signs of conformity in any school group – the way you dress, speak, the bands you like etc.?
- How does the group exert pressure on the individual?
- What kinds of 'different behaviour' are most threatening to the group – what kinds of things does everyone want to keep secret?

JOKES AND REFERENCES

Series 1 Episode 8 'Me Robot – You Jane'.

As well as its allegorical qualities, BTVS demonstrates another feature of certain modern television programmes with its joking references to old films and popular culture generally. The writers enjoy putting together 'real research' into ancient myths and legends and a 'playful' use of popular culture. For most of the audience the title of this episode makes sense because the story is about a demon who gets into a computer network and 'seduces' Willow. But for much older audiences (BTVS is popular across the age range) the title has a much deeper meaning. It refers to a famous science-fiction story from the 1950s called 'I, Robot'. This was a moral story about the 'rules of robot behaviour' (which, of course the demon doesn't follow). The other half of the title refers to the Tarzan novels and films from the early twentieth century with their famous line, 'Me Tarzan, You Jane'. These stories about a macho man and a weak woman are now very out of date and quite the opposite of BTVS, so there is a deep sense of irony in referring to them.

THE CHARACTERS IN BTVS

The other characters in the series are as important as Buffy herself. In the episode referred to above, Willow, Buffy's 'helper' in the war on the demons, gets involved with a computer chatline. Willow is represented as something of a 'plain Jane' (as suggested in the title) who has not had much luck with boyfriends. She fancies Xander, but he is secretly in love with Buffy. When she finds that the chatroom 'boy' is interested in her, she becomes excited and behaves very differently towards Buffy and Xander, unaware that her new admirer is controlled by a demon (who Willow has inadvertently admitted to the computer network).

There is quite a lot more going on in this episode, but Willow's story demonstrates the allegorical dimension. On the one hand, it carries a social message – it's about the dangers of meeting strangers in a chatroom. But it also explores personal issues – Willow is so anxious that she should have a boyfriend that she changes her behaviour, becoming quite reckless where she would normally be very cautious. Very often, people who are restrained most of the time, go 'too far the other way' when the restraints are lifted. This kind of behaviour is common in BTVS, as it is in real life.

3 Look for another episode of BTVS in which Willow is the central character.
- Do Willow's actions in your chosen episode confirm the analysis of her character in 'Me Robot – You Jane' above?
- Does Willow's behaviour in your chosen episode suggest a similar metaphor about teenage problems?

4 What kind of character is Xander?
- Select any episode in which Xander is the central character. What are his usual qualities? How are they used or abused in the story?
- Is it possible to say how stories with Xander offer a form of commentary about the problems of being a young man in contemporary society (ie in the way that Buffy's and Willow's adventures comment on young women's lives)?

ESSAY QUESTIONS & SUGGESTIONS FOR COURSEWORK

The following questions and suggestions will help you to extend work or recast some of the questions in the pack. All of the titles build upon work completed within the case studies for each focus text.

Kes

1 What kind of world is constructed in *Kes*? Write about:
- The ways in which Ken Loach, the film's director, tries to make the film as realistic as possible;
- His choice of actors for certain parts;
- The way in which dialogue is used;
- The settings used in the film, eg school, home, countryside and streets;
- The uses of camera, sound and colour.

Extension work:

How does the representation of Billy Casper's world in the film differ from, or reflect, the world created in A Kestrel for a Knave?

2 Barry Hines says that A Kestrel for A Knave makes people realise that 'it is possible to achieve something in life, however difficult the circumstances.' How are Billy's 'circumstances' expressed within the film? Consider:
- What Billy's difficulties are and how they are represented in the film;
- The extent to which he is successful in overcoming obstacles;
- How the film conveys ideas about 'achieving something in life' and how it represents the impossibility of overcoming some of the social problems explored.

3 How does the way in which the story is filmed help to emphasize the connections between the training of *Kes* and Billy's training for life?
The first part of the Case Study on *Kes* will help you to tackle this question. It will also help if you focus on particular scenes, which seem to illustrate the metaphorical connections between Billy and Kes. Analyse carefully how the film's language helps to express these connections.

4 Compare and contrast the representation of the hero in *Kes* and *The Crucible* (or *To Kill A Mockingbird* or *Pleasantville*). It will help if you consider the following questions:
- Who is the hero? Is he/she a typical film hero? If not, what are the main differences?
- Are we shown the story from the hero's point of view?
- How are the emotions of certain characters expressed? Is it always through body language, facial expressions or dialogue?
- How important is costume or make up?
- Do we feel sympathy for the central characters? How is this sympathy evoked (caused) by the film's language?

5 Discuss the ways in which Ken Loach's use of real pupils and a real school helps to underline important comments made by Barry Hines on the education system. Use the work completed in the central part of the Case Study on Kes to help you with this question. You can also consider the classroom scene that immediately follows the caning of the smokers. Think carefully about the way in which the camera is used to emphasise the reactions of individual students and the importance of Billy.
Other scenes that would be helpful when answering this question are:
- The changing room scene;
- The football match;
- Billy's careers interview.

To Kill A Mockingbird

6 Consider how the metaphor involving the mockingbird helps to draw together the story of *To Kill a Mockingbird* and give it deeper meanings. Look again at the opening sequence and then go back to the work completed at the beginning of the Case Study on this film. Other sequences mentioned in the Case Study will also help, for example, dinner with Walter Cunningham and Scout's conversation with Atticus on the porch which follows; and the sequence near the end during which the Sheriff tells Atticus that he will be treating Bob Ewell's death as an accident.

7 Harper Lee uses both central and minor characters to explore some of the main concerns in her novel. Go back to the Case Study and list what you think are the most important issues dealt with in the film text. Choose three of the following characters from the film and write about the way they are represented: Mrs. Dubose, Walter Cunningham, Mayella Ewell, Bob Ewell, Calpurnia, Boo Radley, Atticus and Scout.

- Consider how effective the representations of these characters are in highlighting the 'main concerns' of the film. Think carefully about:
- Costume and make up
- Body language and facial expressions
- Acting styles
- Dialogue
- Environment (Where do you see these characters? Are they comfortable in their environment? Who are they with? What is the reaction of the other people in the scene to these particular characters?)
- How is the camera used to underline important aspects of these character's personalities?

8 Examine the ways in which the use of metaphor in *Kes* and *To Kill a Mockingbird* helps us to understand the emotional world of the central characters and allows us a greater insight into important themes and issues.

- There is a wealth of information in both Case Studies that you can use when tackling this question. It will help if you look closely at one particular scene from each film in order to illustrate your main points. Remember to examine carefully how every element of the film's language contributes to the overall meaning of the scene.

Pleasantville

9 Using the work completed in your Case Study, discuss how *Pleasantville* uses a fantasy world to explore real world issues.

- You should look at the representation of the fantasy world and compare it with the representation of the real world at the beginning and end of the film. Think carefully about the questions raised by the perfect American sitcom world.

10 ary Ross says that his initial idea for *Pleasantville* was to create a place where there 'is no color, noise, doubt or uncertainty' and to examine what we would have to eliminate in order to achieve it. An important way in which he does this is by the use of contrasts or oppositions. The film language in *Pleasantville* is constantly drawing our attention to a number of these sharp contrasts/oppositions. For example:

- Black-and-white
- Black-and-white and colour
- Freedom and restraint
- Today and yesterday
- Peace and disturbance.

Can you identify any more contrasts? Write about the way in which these are used to highlight important themes and issues in *Pleasantville*.

11 'With our understanding of history we can think about *Pleasantville* in terms of two views of America.' (See the notes in the *Pleasantville* Case Study.) What are these two views? How are they explored in the film? Use your case study to give you the background information needed in order to tackle this question. You will also need to choose particular scenes from the film and examine how these opposing views are represented.

The Crucible

12 *The Crucible* is a film that can be read on a number of different levels. Look carefully at the opening and closing sequences of the film. Write about the ways in which the film's language helps to create atmosphere and convey a number of different meanings to the audience. The detailed work completed in the case study should give you lots of ideas for this question.

13 Discuss the importance of hysteria in *The Crucible*. How is a feeling of growing hysteria created by the film's language? You should consider at least two sequences when tackling this question. The opening scene and the courtroom scene could be used although there are a number of other choices that would be equally helpful. Think carefully about the use of:
- Lighting
- Sound
- Colour
- Camerawork
- Editing
- Mise-en-scéne

14 Both *Pleasantville* and *The Crucible* encourage us to make parallels and connections with issues in today's society. Discuss the ways in which each film makes it hard for us to be satisfied with a simple reading.

The Wizard of Oz

15 *The Wizard of Oz* is not simply a children's film. The representation of the characters and environment can be 'read' on different levels. Using the work completed in your Case Study on this film describe the representation of characters and environment and consider the different meanings they may have.

16 In what ways does Dorothy in *The Wizard of Oz* learn things about herself and about the world generally? Show how the characters she meets offer the audience ideas about universal aspects of human behaviour.

17 How do the music performances (songs and dances) help to produce meaning in *The Wizard of Oz*? Refer in your answer to the use of colour in the staging of these sequences and in establishing the contrast between Oz and Dorothy's home in Kansas.

Buffy the Vampire Slayer

18 *Buffy the Vampire Slayer* has its roots in nineteenth century literature and yet it is still a series about modern teenagers and modern issues. What are the characteristics of the Gothic horror genre used in Buffy and how are they used in a twenty-first century world?

19 *Buffy the Vampire Slayer* is a series that employs some of the features of the 'continuous series'. Show how the series is able to weave together different narrative threads in a single episode and how it enables the characters to grow up and mature over several seasons of shows. Illustrate your answer with references to at least two different episodes from two different seasons.

20 Select one episode of *Buffy the Vampire Slayer* and explain how at least one narrative strand can be seen to work either as an allegory or a moral tale about the social behaviour of young people. Show how this narrative strand interacts with the other stories in the episode.

RESOURCES

CINEMA SCREENINGS

Taking students to a cinema screening has several major benefits. Most video systems are incapable of reproducing the full experience of a film screening and certainly not the full range of film language (especially film sound and the intricacies of colour). A continuous screening in a large auditorium is also much more motivating for students. Video is then extremely useful for follow-up work.

The network of regional film theatres and other cinemas run by local authorities are keen to work with schools on education projects, as are some local commercial cinemas. Cinemas can book films for 'education only' showings at a reduced rate and it is possible to screen films in the morning at reasonable rates – especially if a whole year group attends or perhaps classes from two or more local schools. Some cinemas may also be able to find someone to introduce the film or talk to students afterwards.

A list of independent cinemas likely to offer such screenings is given on the bfi website at www.bfi.org.uk. In the case of other local cinemas, the manager should be approached directly.

AVAILABILITY OF TITLES

All of the films covered in this pack were available on video and DVD at the time of writing.

Buffy The Vampire Slayer (TV series 1997–present) is available in various collections on video and DVD (but note that from Series 3 these are certificated at '15'). BBC2 re-runs the earlier series as well as following Sky One with the later series. On BBC2 a lightly censored version is broadcast in the early evening with the full version shown late at night. The first two series deal with Buffy's adventures in high school – she then moves on to college.

One other film that could easily be used as an alternative to the selections in the pack is *The Mighty* (US, 1998). Based on the young person's novel of the same name by Rodman Philbrick this tells the story of two thirteen-year-old boys, one of whom is disabled by a wasting disease and the other who is physically strong but has a learning disability. The narrative connects the fantasy world of medieval knights with the realities of inner-city life. The strong cast includes Sharon Stone and Gillian Anderson in small roles.

INTERNET RESEARCH

Much of the research for this pack was undertaken on the internet and students could usefully find much of the material themselves. Some useful sites are:

The Wizard of Oz

http://www.halcyon.com/piglet/Populism.htm
http://people.cornell.edu/pages/dbj5/oz.html
http://www.geocities.com/Hollywood/Hills/6396/ozcritic.htm
These sites all carry very interesting material on the various theories as to the allegorical meaning of the Frank L. Baum's writings about Oz.

Buffy the Vampire Slayer

http://www.buffyguide.com
http://www.bbc.co.uk/cult/buffy/
http://www.buffyworld.com/slanguage/index.htm
There are many Buffy fansites and episode guides. They are useful in finding descriptions of the 'backstory' (ie what has happened before a specific episode) and boning up on the characters and their unusual speech and behaviour.

The Crucible

http://www.sdcoe.k12.ca.us/score/cruc/cructg.html
http://www.teachtheteachers.org/projects/AMoore/Crucible.htm
http://www.ogram.org/17thc/fact-fiction.shtml
As a major work on the US school curriculum, *The Crucible* figures heavily on the web. The first two sites here are US school resources with good links to other websites. The third site is a rather tetchy response to Arthur Miller with a detailed historical account of the actual Salem trials. This might be useful in alerting students to the difference between 'history' and 'allegory'.

To Kill a Mockingbird

http://www.webenglishteacher.com/lee.html
memory.loc.gov/ammem/ndlpedu/lessons/98/mock/intro.html
http://www.filmsite.org/toki3.html

As with *The Crucible*, there are many websites designed to help English teachers in American classrooms. The first site here includes a good selection of links to relevant material. The third site offers a detailed review/synopsis of the film, which is useful in indicating sequences that repay close study (including the brilliant opening credit sequence).

Kes

http://www.filmeducation.org/secondary/s_archive/rep/main_1.html
Film Education provide an online resource pack of material on films associated with 'Representations of Youth' – *Kes* is one of the featured films.
http://www.geocities.com/freycinette/Kes.html
This site listed here offers a number of resources, including a link to a useful Guardian article with interviews with some of the main contributors to the film.

Pleasantville

http://www.primalspirit.com/muse_pleasantville.htm
This site offers an essay on how *Pleasantville* can be read as an historical allegory and how it demonstrates the rise to power of the 'Sixties Generation' at the expense of the 'Forties Generation'. It also makes links to the Beatles' film The Yellow Submarine (*Pleasantville* ends with the Beatles song 'Across the Universe'.
http://www.cnn.com/SHOWBIZ/Movies/9810/12/austin.ross/index.html
This site offers an interview with writer/director Gary Ross.

Please remember that web addresses are liable to change at any time. All of the above were 'live' when these notes were written, but they could well have 'died' by the time you try to reach them. It is usually possible to find all the material you want via a simple search using Google (www.google.co.uk). Just type in the title of the film and perhaps one other word such as 'allegory' or the name of the director.

OTHER TEACHING MATERIALS

The first Teaching Pack in this series from bfi/itp is *Reading Films*, which includes work on *Clueless*, *Pretty in Pink* and television soap operas, as well as *Kes* and *Pleasantville*. The focus is on the use of film language and the development of film narratives.

Also from the bfi comes *Moving Images in the Classroom* and the CD-ROM, *An Introduction to Film Language*. See www.bfi.org.uk/education for details.

in the picture publishes a pack of materials on the genre of 'Youth Pix'. Although originally written for A Level students, these can be adapted for use with KS4. (See the website at www.itpmag.demon.co.uk.)

TEXT BOOKS

There are several textbooks written for GCSE Media Studies which might be useful for your students:

Julian Bowker (2002) *Looking at Media Studies for GCSE*, Hodder & Stoughton Educational
Vivienne Clark and Richard Harvey (eds) (2002) *GCSE Media Studies*, Longman Education
Mike Edwards, Barbara Connell, Jude Brigley (2000) *Investigating Media Studies*, Hodder & Stoughton Educational
Peter Wall and Paul Walker (2002) *Media Studies for GCSE*, Collins Educational

You may find the following A Level textbooks useful as a source of further ideas about the concepts of narrative, genre and representation:

Gill Branston and Roy Stafford (2002, 3rd ed) *The Media Student's Book*, Routledge
Nick Lacey (2000) *Narrative and Genre*, Palgrave
Nick Lacey (1998) *Image and Representation*, Palgrave
Colin Stewart, Marc Lavelle and Adam Kowaltze (2001), *Media and Meaning*, British Film Institute

The Media Student's Book includes a case study on *Buffy the Vampire Slayer* as well as an extensive bibliography of academic work on the series.